Roni Rosenthal-Gazit

101 (one o one)
- Let's have fun -

101 fun activities that reinforce learning in the Hebrew Language

Plus more than 30 worksheets in Hebrew

A Special Edition for Hebrew/Jewish School Teachers

101 - Let's have fun

101 fun activities that reinforce learning in the Hebrew Language

A Special Edition for Hebrew/Jewish School Teachers
Copyright © 2009 Roni Rosenthal-Gazit

Published by StoryTime World – Publishing house
5268G Nicholson Lane, Suite 380
Kensington, MD, 20895
info@101letshavefun.com
202-4360786
www.storytimeworld.com
www.101letshavefun.com

Printed in the United States of America.

Library of Congress Number: 2009900134   ISBN: 978-0-9792800-1-6

StoryTime World - publishing house

Dedication

This book is dedicated to my sister (yes, Miki, to you!)
For always being there for me...

TABLE OF CONTENTS

Introduction

? **Have** you ever felt that when you teach kids a new concept in Hebrew the kids are not really there with you?

? **Have** you ever felt that you have covered a lot of material in one day and both you and the students need to lighten things up and have some fun?

? **Have** you ever had the feeling that you are not sure if the students really understand the material and you are looking for a new way to reinforce vocabulary?

? **Have** you ever felt that the students are full of energy and need to calm down before you can start teaching?

? **Have** you ever realized that you have just 5-10 minutes until the end of the lesson and you just want to lighten the mood and play something fun with the kids?

? **How** about an introduction to games at the beginning of the year?

? **How** about a fun way to practice and play some games?

? **How** about teaching new vocabulary through games?

? **How** about just having fun in Hebrew?

? **Are** you tired of asking the kids "Tell me 2 new things you've learned today"?

Learning through games is an experience that kids will never forget. The words they learn while playing will stay in their minds for a long, long time. Yes, learning Hebrew can be fun. Actually learning any language can be fun. You just have to make it… fun.

Hello, my name is Roni and I am a teacher.

Over the years I have collected over 1000 (!) games.

In this book I would like to share with you the ones I graded as 'my 101 top list'. The games in this book were the most popular, captured the interest of my students and made them want to participate. Above all, through the use of these games I was always able to teach the kids something new; sometimes it was new vocabulary or reinforcement of basic words, and other times I helped the students grow more confident with conversational Hebrew.

I started working with kids as a guide when I was 16 years old and was given my first group with the youth movement HATZOFIM (a group of Israeli scouts).

Even now, after many years of teaching in formal and non-formal structures, in Hebrew schools and Jewish schools, teaching kids at different levels of the Hebrew language and different grades from pre-k through 8th grade, I still believe that the best way for a child or an adult to get a feel for a language is by playing games.

A person walks into a restaurant, sits down, and asks for a menu. After a careful review of the menu, he will probably pick something and order it. Chances are, he will not remember that menu again, but he will definitely remember eating at that restaurant, maybe the name of the dish he liked, and he may even remember how it tastes. The next time he walks into this restaurant he will feel more comfortable reading the menu and trying to remember what he ordered before.

Children experience much the same thing. When children have enjoyed playing a certain game in Hebrew, they will ask to play it again and again. They will remember having fun but most importantly they will feel comfortable using Hebrew vocabulary as a means for playing games. In game playing children's imaginations are hard at work. They will conceive variations of words, symbols, and meanings as well as basic vocabulary while acquiring new language skills, all by playing games.

How To Use This Book

Most of the games presented in this book do not need any prior preparation (and if they do, it's minimal). Most of the games do not require the use of any special materials, other than basic things you can find in any classroom (such as paper, scissors, pencils, a ball, or pictures of objects you can print from the internet).

I have also tried to divide the games into grades. Use this simply as a guide, there are no hard and fast rules. A teacher is the best judge of whether a game is suitable for their class. If you think the kids will enjoy it, go for it, no matter what their age.

As a teacher, I found it very helpful to keep a 'prize box' next to my desk. Prizes, such as lollipops, stickers, balloons or crayons, will do the job!

Acknowledgment

I want to thank colleagues and students for the hundreds of hours spent wisely and fruitfully searching for new games. I want to thank my family, my mom and dad; my spouse Gilad and my wonderful kids Shachar and Lior (Kiki). I want to thank Miki, Ronen, Gal, Noy, Jen and Yam. A special thanks to Hadass Rosenthal, Marina Kraus, Yaniv Barad, Natan Fingerman and Jova Mirona for making this book happen. Thank you all for your support, help, brainstorming, and patience. Thank you for being my audience.

So grab the book and let's play…

Enjoy.

P.S. I know for a fact that there are many other games up for grabs. If you are a teacher, a parent, or a student and would like to share your ideas with me, I would love to hear from you. Send communications to me via email at: RoniRG@101letshavefun.com. Thank you.

Game no. 1
The Color Game

Objective:	practice colors in Hebrew
Suitable for Grades:	K – 4th
Playing Time:	5 – 7 Minutes
Materials:	None
Grouping/Organization:	Large group
Variations:	Use simple colors for Kindergartners and more complex colors for older students

Helpful Hints:

This game works great as practice after teaching the colors first, or at the beginning of the year to refresh students' minds about the names of the colors.

How to Play:

The teacher calls the name of a color (for example: yellow) in Hebrew. The kids run to a yellow object in the classroom and touch it. The game can be played in class or outside in a playground. If playing outside, make sure there are enough colorful objects around to make the game work.

A variation:

If a student gets confused they can sit out, get a second chance, or just sit out for 2 minutes, and then come back to the game.

A safety tip:

I recommend against allowing children to touch each other's clothing, shoes, etc. even if it matches the color called. It is better to touch only objects or pictures.

Game no. 2
The Shapes Game

Objective:	To practice shapes in Hebrew
Suitable for Grades:	K - 3rd
Playing Time:	5 – 7 Minutes
Materials:	None
Grouping/Organization:	Large group
Variations:	Simple shapes for Kindergartners; more complex shapes for older students.

Helpful Hints:

It is best to teach the shapes first, or refresh students' knowledge of shapes prior to playing the game. Then use the game as practice for reinforcement.

How to Play:

The teacher calls the name of a shape in Hebrew. The kids then run to an object in the classroom, (that is the shape called), and touch it. The game can be played in class or outside in a playground. If playing outside, make sure there are enough objects to match the shapes to make the game work.

A variation:

A useful variation is to combine colors and shapes. For example, the teacher can call: "Touch a blue triangle," "a red square," etc.

Game no. 3
It's My Face/Body

Objective:	To practice the parts of the face and body in Hebrew
Suitable for Grades:	K - 3rd
Playing Time:	5 – 7 Minutes
Materials:	None
Grouping/Organization:	Large group
Variations:	Major face and body parts for kindergartners, more complex face and body parts for older students

Helpful Hints:

This game works best as practice and reinforcement after teaching the face and body parts.

How to Play:

This is a combination of the color game and "Simon says." The teacher will touch a face or body part, and the kids will touch the corresponding face or body part on their own body, but only when the teacher says "Simon says." If the teacher touches a body part and does not say "Simon says," the students are not to touch their own body part. This game gets really funny when the teacher tries to confuse the students by touching an ear and saying "Simon says touch your nose".

A variation:

I would recommend instructing students not to touch their friend's face.

Game no. 4
Taboo Words

Objective:	To practice basic conversational vocabulary in Hebrew
Suitable for Grades:	3rd – 6th
Playing Time:	5 – 7 Minutes
Materials:	Flash cards for option 1, no materials needed for option 2
Grouping/Organization:	Large group

TABOO WORDS:
FLOWER,
PERFUMED

Helpful Hints:

The flash cards should include the picture of an object along with "taboo" words. For example, a banana can include the words "yellow" and "fruit" as taboo words. Every object will have its own list of taboo words. Students will remember these taboo words forever.

How to Play:

There are 2 options to play this game:

Option 1: Show the students a flash card of an object. Ask a "volunteer" to describe this object to the class without using the "Taboo" words.

Option 2: The teacher or a "volunteer" asks each student a question. Each student has to answer the question without using the "Taboo" words. If you are not using flashcards, you can simply write the taboo words on the board. Taboo words for this option could be for example, "Yes," "No," "Blue," "White", or other words of your choosing.

TABOO WORDS:
YELLOW, FRUIT

TABOO WORDS:
MOUSE, ANIMAL

TABOO WORDS:
RED, TOMATO

Game no. 5
Prepositions: Is it "in" or "on"

Objective:	To practice prepositions
Suitable for Grades:	3rd – 6th
Playing Time:	5 – 7 Minutes
Materials:	None
Grouping/Organization:	2 Groups (example: boys vs. girls)

Helpful Hints:

Ask a student to act out as you say a sentence in Hebrew. For example, they might place a book on the table, under a table, or in a box etc. as they use the prepositions in a sentence. In this way they use the prepositions (ב, על, תחת, על יד, בין ועוד).

Later, read a simple text (with prepositions) and see what a difference it makes.

How to Play:

Split the class into 2-3 groups, and start giving instructions similar to the following "Group 1: crawl under the chairs please"; Group 2: "sit on the desks please"; Group 3: "stand next to the board etc". It's important to give each group one instruction and move to the next group so that no group waits too long.

A good way to create the groups is simply boys vs. girls, or all those with birthdays from October to March and then those with birthdays from April to September.

Game no. 6
Animals or Else...

Objective:	To learn the names of animals in Hebrew
Suitable for Grades:	K - 3rd
Playing Time:	7 – 12 Minutes
Materials:	Pictures of animals or animal figures (toys)
Grouping/Organization:	Large group

Helpful Hints:

This is a nice activity in which your students will laugh a lot.

How to Play:

Introduce each animal by name (Hebrew and English) to the students and add their respective sounds. (Remember a duck in Hebrew goes Ga-Ga, and a frog goes Qua-qua, and a rooster goes Ku-Ku-Ri-Ku-Ku).

After this introduction ask one volunteer to act out the sound of an animal. The students have to guess the name of the animal in Hebrew.

Game no. 7
Hot or Cold

Objective:	To practice the terms hot and cold in Hebrew as well as Hebrew vocabulary
Suitable for Grades:	K - 3rd
Playing Time:	5 – 10 Minutes
Materials:	None
Grouping/Organization:	Large group

Helpful Hints:

A nice game for the end of the lesson

How to Play:

Ask a volunteer to leave the class. Ask the students to pick one object that everybody agrees on. The students should know the name of the object in Hebrew.

Call back the volunteer. The volunteer has to guess the object by walking slowly around the room making guesses.

When they move near the object their classmates will scream "hot", but if they move away from the object their classmates will scream "cold". You can limit the volunteer to only 5 guesses or the game can drag out.

Game no. 8
Play the Song

Objective:	To enrich Hebrew vocabulary by using real objects
Suitable for Grades:	3rd – 6th.
Playing Time:	12 - 15 Minutes
Materials:	Hebrew songs
Grouping/Organization:	2 - 3 Groups

Helpful Hints:
This game can get noisy but it is very funny.

How to Play:
Split the class into 2-3 groups. Give each group a different song in Hebrew on a CD. Help them understand the words. It's important to make sure that each song has many "touchable" items.
Ask the student to not only to learn to sing the song but also make up motions to their song by acting out the words. For example, for a "home" they can make the shape of a "roof", and for "dog" they can "bark" etc.
Give them 10 minutes to practice their song prior to performing it in front of the class.
Enjoy!

Game no. 9
Around the World (Letters/Words)

Objective:	To practice the alphabet or to practice Hebrew vocabulary and reading simple words and sentences
Suitable for Grades:	K – 6th
Playing Time:	7 – 10 Minutes
Materials:	None
Grouping/Organization:	Large group

Helpful Hints:

This game is a great way to review letters, words, and a quick way to learn how to read.

How to Play:

Ask one student to stand next to a friend. Ask a question aimed at those 2 students. The first to yell the correct answer moves up ιo the next student. The one who misses out takes his friend's seat until the end of the game.

You can simply ask the question, "What letter follows the letter 'x'?" You can also write a letter on the board and ask students to read it by asking "What sound does this letter make?" or "Give me a word that starts with this letter?" You can also write words on the board and ask the students to pronounce the words, with or without vowels.

For a more advanced version of the game ask "How do you say "a ball" in Hebrew?" Or ask questions related to a word, phrase, or sentence that you write on the board in print or script.

Game no. 10
Tag The Story

Objective:	To practice conversational skills in Hebrew
Suitable for Grades:	K – 6th
Playing Time:	10 – 12 Minutes
Materials:	None
Grouping/Organization:	Large group

Helpful Hints:

This is a great game to get students moving around.

How to Play:

One volunteer gets to be "it". The "Tagger" needs to run around and tries to touch someone else. If they succeed, the tagged student must freeze and begin telling a story in Hebrew, until they say "MILCHAMA" (מלחמה), (tag war). At that point the tagged student runs around and tags another student in order to keep the story going in Hebrew. The student who successfully tags their replacement can go back to the game.

Game no. 11
Bingo

Objective:	To learn and practice new Hebrew vocabulary
Suitable for Grades:	3rd – 6th
Playing Time:	10 – 15 Minutes
Materials:	A sheet of paper with a 4 x 4 grid
Grouping/Organization:	Large group

Helpful Hints:

This game is a great review of vocabulary and writing skills. A handy tip is to have lollipops or other prizes handy for the winners. You can play until there are 3-4 winners or until everybody wins.

How to Play:

Begin by writing 25 words on the board and then ask the students to pick just 16 out of them and copy them into the table above (one word in each square).

Write the words on individual pieces of paper and fold them into two.

Ask a student to pick one folded note from the pile of words. (The teacher can also do this part without the help of a student if you prefer). Unfold the paper and read it aloud. All the students who have this word on their chart write an X on it.

Then pick the next word, and so on. The students who complete one line of words (read aloud), or in a diagonal line call "BINGO."

Words can be for example: Any color, shape, season, holiday, and more.

אִשָּׁה	בַּיִת	שׁוּלְחָן	תַּפּוּחַ
(woman)	(house)	(table)	(apple)
חָתוּל	שֶׁמֶשׁ	עֵץ	צַעֲצוּעַ
(cat)	(sun)	(tree)	(toy)
יָדִיד	אֶרֶץ	זֶבְרָה	עַכְבָּר
(friend)	(country)	(zebra)	(mouse)
דָּג	הַר	עֵץ	סֵפֶר
(fish)	(mountain)	(tree)	(book)

Game no. 12
Is It On Your Back?

Objective:	To practice Hebrew vocabulary
Suitable for Grades:	3rd – 6th
Playing Time:	10 – 12 Minutes
Materials:	Small pictures of objects and some tape
Grouping/Organization:	Large group
Variations:	For older kids you can refer to abstract items such as noise, voice, and spirit.

Helpful Hints:

This game is ideal for reviewing Hebrew and symbolic words for holidays.

How to Play:

A volunteer student is asked to step outside. Show the remaining students a picture of a single item. Call the volunteer back into the classroom. Tape the picture to his/her back so he/she can't see it. The volunteer asks questions in Hebrew to find out what the picture is. The other students are only allowed to answer "yes" or "no."

You can limit the game to 15 or so questions according to the amount of time available for playing the game.

Game no. 13
Memory Game (Words, Phrases, Questions)

Objective:	To practice Hebrew vocabulary and reading simple and complex sentences or words
Suitable for Grades:	K – 6th
Playing Time:	10 – 12 Minutes
Materials:	Flash cards with pictures and the corresponding Hebrew word, or flash cards with phrases split into two parts (the first half on one card and the second half on another card), or questions on one card and a matching answer on another
Grouping/Organization:	3 – 4 Small Groups
Variations:	You can also play the game in a large group and let each student in the group have one turn.

Helpful Hints:
This is a great way of reviewing vocabulary or teaching new phrases. Keep the groups small, with no more than 4-5 kids in each.

How to Play:
Divide the class into 3-4 groups, with no more than 4-5 kids in each group.
Spread the cards face down. Each student in the group gets one turn.
They each pick 2 cards and find a match between an object and its translation in Hebrew, or 2 cards and find a match between the first and second part of the phrase, or find the correct answer to a specific question.

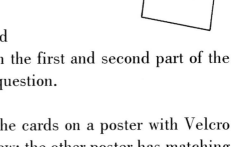

Another way to play this game is by hanging the cards on a poster with Velcro tape. One poster has cards with words in Hebrew; the other poster has matching cards with pictures. The students take turns to match a word with its translation. This way works well in the big group variation.

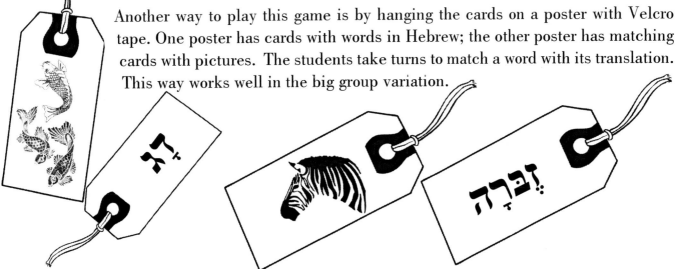

Game no. 14
The Password

Objective:	To practice Hebrew vocabulary
Suitable for Grades:	K – 6th
Playing Time:	10 – 12 Minutes
Materials:	None
Grouping/Organization:	Large group

Helpful Hints:

A good way to get the students moving around while reviewing vocabulary.

How to Play:

Pick 3-4 students to be the "cats" and send them outside, until the class decides on a password. Pick another 3-4 students to be the "mice." The remaining students hold hands and make a circle.

The mice stand in the middle of the circle, and the cats stand outside the circle. When the game starts, the cats need to find out the password in order for the gate to open. The cats get 5 hints from their classmates to guess the word. If the cats guess the correct password, the gates are opened (students making the circle drop their hands) and the mice need to run out and touch the nearest wall before the cats catch them.

If they are caught by a cat, they get to be a cat in the next round and the teacher picks a new mouse to replace them. Cats that catch mice get to return to the circle and join hands. Mice that are not caught or cats that do not catch mice get to keep their positions in the next round.

Game no. 15
1, 2, 3 Move

Objective:	To practice the sounds of the Hebrew letters
Suitable for Grades:	2nd – 5th
Playing Time:	5 – 7 Minutes
Materials:	None
Grouping/Organization:	Large group

1, 2, 3 ...

Helpful Hints:

This game is suitable for the end of the lesson or when the students are restless and need to move around. Make sure tables and chairs are moved aside so there is plenty of space to play.

How to Play:

Students are standing in a line, at the back of the room and facing the board. The teacher (or a volunteer) is standing on the other side of the class. The teacher and students agree on a common sign, for example, when the teacher says words that begin with the letter "Het" in Hebrew.

The teacher closes his/her eyes and counts as fast as they can - 1,2,3 and a word that begins with the letter "Het." The students are expected to move forward until the teacher opens her/his eyes. When the teacher does so, everybody freezes. If someone moves after the teacher has opened his/her eyes, that student has to go back back 3 steps.

The teacher can try to confuse the students by saying words that do not begin with "Het" (but might sound similar.) The winner is the first student who crosses the room to the other side.

Game no. 16
You've Got Mail!

Objective:	To practice reading, comprehension and conversational Hebrew
Suitable for Grades:	4th – 6th
Playing Time:	10 – 15 Minutes
Materials:	A packet (a prize wrapped in layers of newspaper or wrapping paper) and cards with questions, phrases or small tasks in Hebrew)
Grouping/Organization:	Large group
Variations:	Instead of questions on the card, the cards contain the second half of a phrase or an assignment that students have to complete, such as checking their reading level etc.

Helpful Hints:

This game is great as an introductory game at the beginning of the year or for periodic evaluation of the student's level of comprehension in Hebrew.

How to Play:

The teacher takes a small prize (eraser, lollipop, etc.) and wraps it in layers, in old newspapers, reused wrapping paper, or something similar. The teacher tapes a small card on each layer with a question in Hebrew, an assignment or half of a phrase, for example:

- **What's your favorite color?**
- **Walk 3 laps around the room, etc.**

The students sit in a circle and pass the packet around to each other. When the teacher claps his/her hands the student who has the packet reads the question in Hebrew and tries to answer it. If **they can read** the card, understand the question, and answer correctly in Hebrew they get to peel the first layer of the packet revealing the next card. The students then continue passing the packet till the teacher claps again. If a student **can't read**, doesn't understand, or can't answer (depending on the level of the class) that student doesn't get to peel a layer, and just passes the package along.

Game no. 17
Know Your Letter

Objective:	To practice Hebrew letters
Suitable for Grades:	K – 1st
Playing Time:	5 – 7 Minutes
Materials:	Flash cards with the Hebrew alphabet (in script or print)
	2 Groups
Grouping/Organization:	

Helpful Hints:

This game is good for practice at the beginning of the lesson, review at the beginning of the year or following a break from school. Make sure each group gets identical sets of flash cards.

How to Play:

The teacher divides the class into two groups, and gives each group flash cards with Hebrew letters. The teacher announces the name of a letter. The first student who has the flash card with the announced letter (2 students should have it, one in each group) needs to run to the teacher and hand in the announced flash card, and goes back to his seat. The winner's group earns 1 point and the team with the most points wins.

Game no. 18
Script Print Match

Objective:	To practice Hebrew letters in script and print
Suitable for Grades:	K – 1st
Playing Time:	5 – 7 Minutes
Materials:	Flash cards with the Hebrew alphabet in script and print.
Grouping/Organization:	2 Groups

Helpful Hints:
Good for practice at the beginning of the year or to practice the letters at any time.

How to Play:
The teacher divides the class into two groups. Each group gets two sets of the Hebrew letters, one in print and one in script. The students need to match the letters in print with those in script. The group that finishes first is the winner.

Game no. 19
Let's Count - Numbers

Objective:	To practice counting numbers in Hebrew
Suitable for Grades:	K (numbers up to 10) - 3rd (Numbers up to 100)
Playing Time:	5 – 7 Minutes
Materials:	A ball or a marker
Grouping/Organization:	Large group
Variations:	Have the students count up to a certain number, such as 30, and then start over, or count back from 30 to 1.

Helpful Hints:

This game can be played a couple of times during the year until everybody learns the numbers.

How to Play:

Students sit in a big circle. The teacher explains and demonstrates the principle of counting in Hebrew. The teacher passes a marker or a ball to the first student. The first student says the number "one" and passes the ball or marker to their right or left. The students continue to pass the ball or marker from one to the other while counting, so the next student will say the number "two", the third the number "three" and so on.

If someone gets confused they have to leave the circle or just sit out for 2 minutes and then come back.

Game no. 20
Let's Count – Days of the Week/The Jewish Month Calendar

Objective:	To practice the days of the week or counting the month in the Jewish calendar in Hebrew
Suitable for Grades:	K – 1st
Playing Time:	5 – 7 Minutes
Materials:	A ball or a marker
Grouping/Organization:	Large group
Variations:	The teacher can start counting with a different day/month, or count back from Saturday (the last day of the week) or Elul (the last month of the Jewish year).

Helpful Hints:

This game can be played a couple of times during the year until everybody learns the names of the days/months.

How to Play:

The students sit in a big circle. The teacher first explains and demonstrates the principle of counting the days of the week or the Jewish calendar in Hebrew. The teacher passes a marker or a ball to the first student and says: "Sunday" (Yom RISHON), or "Tishrei" (the first month). The student has to pass the item (a marker or a ball) to the student sitting next to them in the circle and say "Monday" (Yom SHENI) or "Cheshvan", and so on.

If someone gets confused they can leave the circle, or just sit out for 2 minutes and then come back.

Game no. 21
The Names Game

Objective:	To practice basic Hebrew vocabulary
Suitable for Grades:	K – 3rd
Playing Time:	5 – 7 Minutes
Materials:	A ball for each group
Grouping/Organization:	2 Groups

Helpful Hints:

A very funny game, great for the beginning of the year.

How to Play:

Divide the class into 2 groups. Give each group a ball. Each student picks an object in Hebrew (for example: שולחן, פרח etc.) they identify with. That will be their "name."

One student throws the ball to the sky and calls out an object. The student who hears their "name" must catch the ball. If they miss 3 times, the group must change that student's name and pick a "new" name for them.

If they catch the ball, it becomes their turn to throw it to the sky and call out another student's name.

Game no. 22
Directions

Objective:	To learn and practice directions in Hebrew
Suitable for Grades:	3rd – 6th
Playing Time:	5 – 7 Minutes
Materials:	None
Grouping/Organization:	Large group

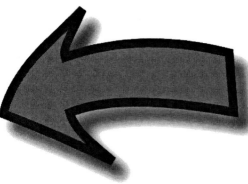

Helpful Hints:

This is a fun game when the students need to move around.

How to Play:

The students stand in a line. The teacher calls for a volunteer to act out the directions with the teacher's help (the teacher may need to translate).

The teacher calls: KADIMA (forward), everybody takes one step forward.
The teacher calls: ACHORA (back), everybody takes one step back.
The teacher calls: YEMINA (right), everybody takes one step to the right.
The teacher calls: SMOLA (left), everybody takes one step to the left.
The teacher calls: LEMALA (up), everybody looks up.
The teacher calls: LEMATA (down), everybody looks down.
Every now and then the teacher should repeat the same instruction twice and try to get the students confused. Whoever gets confused leaves the circle, or just sits out for 2 minutes and then comes back.

Game no. 23
Yam/Yabasha

Objective:	To practice Hebrew vocabulary
Suitable for Grades:	K – 6th
Playing Time:	10 – 12 Minutes
Materials:	None
Grouping/Organization:	Large group

Helpful Hints:

This a fun way to learn more vocabulary, especially opposite words, with some movement.

How to Play:

The students stand in a circle. When the teacher calls: "Yam" (ocean/sea), everybody jumps into the circle and pretends to swim by making swimming movements with their arms. When the teacher calls: "Yabasha" (land), everybody jumps back out of the circle.

A variation:

The teacher can change the words. For example, when the teacher says: «GAVOHA,» (גבוה) (tall) everybody jumps into the circle and walks using both legs; when the teacher calls: "NAMUCH" (נמוך) (short) everybody jumps back and bend down. When the teachers calls out "YAMIN" (ימין) all the students put inside the circle their right hand, and when the teacher calls out "SMOLL" (שמאל) the students put in their left hand, etc'. For older students the teacher can make the game more complicated. For example, when the teacher calls out plural words in Hebrew everybody jumps into the circle, and when they calls out singular words, everybody jumps back from the circle, etc.

Game no. 24
Yom, Yom, Shavuah (Day, Day, Week)

Objective:	To practice basic Hebrew words
Suitable for Grades:	K – 1st
Playing Time:	5 – 7 Minutes
Materials:	None
Grouping/Organization:	Large group

Helpful Hints:

This is a nice game for moving around.

How to Play:

The students sit in a circle. One volunteer has to tap each student on the head and say the same word over and over. After a while the student tapping says a different word. Upon hearing the different word, the student whose head is tapped jumps from their seat and runs after the head-tapper trying to catch them. The head-tapper runs as fast as they can and attempts to take the runner's seat.

Ask the students to change the words with each person's turn.

Game no. 25
Just Act It Out

Objective:	To practice Hebrew vocabulary, words and phrases
Suitable for Grades:	3rd – 8th
Playing Time:	10 - 12 Minutes
Materials:	None
Grouping/Organization:	Large group

Helpful Hints:
This game is great for reviewing new vocabulary and phrases.

How to Play:
The teacher writes new words on the board. Between 10 and 20 words work best. Then the teacher chooses a volunteer and asks them to pick one word out of this list, and act it out, like charades. The other students guess what the word is in Hebrew. Older students can act out phrases with 3-4 or more words.

Game no. 26
It's One Big Word

Objective:	To practice Hebrew vocabulary
Suitable for Grades:	5th – 8th
Playing Time:	15 – 20 Minutes
Materials:	None
Grouping/Organization:	3 – 4 Small groups

Helpful Hints:

It is useful if you have a dictionary handy to use in this game.

How to Play:

Divide the class into 3-4 groups, no more than 4-5 kids in each group.

Each group gets a long word in Hebrew, for example: ENCIKLOPEDIA (אנציקלופדיה), (Encyclopedia), ONEVERSITA (אוניברסיטה) (university), etc. Each group needs to come up with as many words as possible that are "hiding" in this word, using only the Hebrew letters in this long word. The winning group is the one that comes up with most of the new words that are "hiding" in the long word.

Game no. 27
Hang Man

Objective:	To practice Hebrew spelling and decoding
Suitable for Grades:	K – 3rd
Playing Time:	10 - 12 Minutes
Materials:	None
Grouping/Organization:	Large group

Helpful Hints:

This game provides a great way to review letters or teach new phrases.

How to Play:

Ask a student to come up with a word they have recently learned and whisper it in your ear. Write one dash on the board for each letter of the word or words chosen. Don't forget to leave space between words. The students need to guess one letter at a time until they find the right word(s). Fill in the letter (everywhere it appears) on the dash or dashes each time the person guesses correctly. Start drawing a hangman every time a student does not guess correctly. Begin by drawing a head attached to the short vertical line. You can add eyes, ears, nose, hair, body, legs, arms, etc. If the drawing is completed before the students guess the correct word they lose a point. If they guess the word before the picture is complete they win a point.

אַהֲ_ת הַ_הֶ וּלֶ_ת

Game no. 28
Words, More Words

Objective:	To practice reading and writing in Hebrew
Suitable for Grades:	1st – 3rd
Playing Time:	10 – 12 Minutes
Materials:	None
Grouping/Organization:	Large group

Helpful Hints:

Students will benefit from using a dictionary in this game.

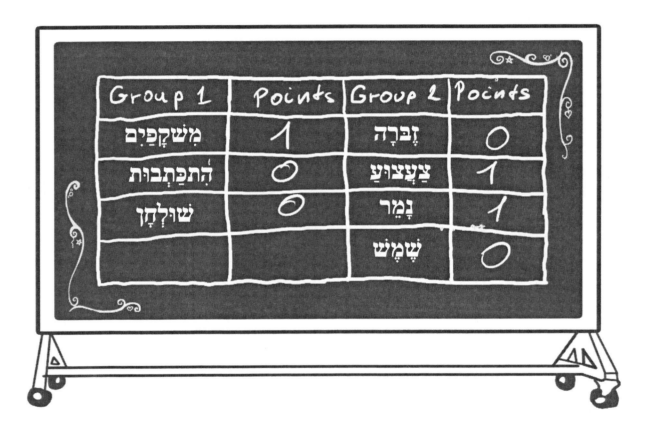

How to Play:

Divide the class into 2 groups. Group number 1 writes one word on the board that Group number 2 has to read. Then switch groups. Group number 2 then writes a word on the board for Group 1 to read. Each group that reads the word correctly gets a point.

Game no. 29
Make It Into A Sentence

Objective:	To practice Hebrew reading, writing and vocabulary
Suitable for Grades:	K – 5th
Playing Time:	5 – 12 Minutes
Materials:	Paper, pencils, pictures of objects, or items you have in class.
Grouping/Organization:	3 – 4 Groups
Variations:	See below

Helpful Hints:

This game is a good way to review basic prepositions and how to interconnect words.

How to Play:

Divide the class into 3-4 groups. Ask each group to write 3 words in Hebrew on a piece of paper. Switch the papers between the groups. Now, ask each group to add only 3 words to make a real sentence. The winner is the group whose sentence is logical, correct, and funny.

A variation:

Divide the class into 3-4 small groups. Give each group 2 pictures of objects, or real items they already know how to identify and say in Hebrew. Ask each group to write a basic sentence using those two objects. For example: "This is a dog and a cat". Now, switch the pictures or objects between the groups so that each group gets 2 more objects or pictures. Ask the students to continue their sentence. For example: "The boy loves the dog, the girl likes the cat".

Game no. 30
The Detective Game

Objective:	To practice Hebrew decoding
Suitable for Grades:	3rd – 6th
Playing Time:	5 – 10 Minutes
Materials:	Paper and pencils
Grouping/Organization:	2 Groups

Helpful Hints:

This is a great way to review basic vocabulary.

How to Play:

Divide the class into 2 groups. Each group writes one scrambled word for the other group. Switch papers. Now each group gets only one minute to find the right word. Start with 3 letter words and keep on playing the game gradually building up to sentences (depending on the level of the class).

Game no. 31
The Telephone

Objective:	To practice Hebrew vocabulary
Suitable for Grades:	K – 1st
Playing Time:	5 Minutes
Materials:	None
Grouping/Organization:	Large group

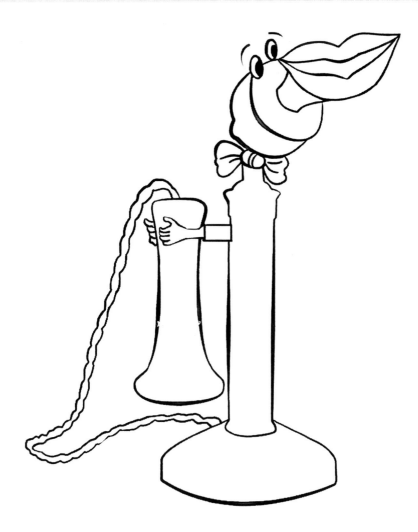

Helpful Hints:

This game gets very funny.

How to Play:

The students sit in a circle quietly. The first student comes up with a word in Hebrew and whispers it in the ear of the student sitting next to them. The second student whispers the same word that he heard in the ear of the third student, and so on. Each student tries to whisper the same word that he heard without changing it. The last student in the circle speaks the word out loud and the students compare it with the original word.

Game no. 32
True or False?

Objective:	To practice conversational Hebrew
Suitable for Grades:	3rd – 8th
Playing Time:	5 – 10 Minutes
Materials:	None
Grouping/Organization:	Individual

Helpful Hints:

This game can sometimes take a long time. I recommend picking out 4 or 5 kids to play the game and let the other students be guessers.

How to Play:

Ask the students to think about 3 sentences they want to say about themselves. 1 out of the 3 sentences must be true, but the other 2 sentences must be false. The rest of the students in class need to guess which one of the sentences is the true one. Of course, the sentences are said in Hebrew.

Game no. 33
From Letters to Words

Objective:	To practice Hebrew vocabulary
Suitable for Grades:	K – 6th (Simple words for K, complex words and sentences for 6th)
Playing Time:	5 – 10 Minutes
Materials:	None
Grouping/Organization:	Large group

Helpful Hints:

This game gets very funny.

How to Play:

The teacher, or a volunteer, comes up with riddles in Hebrew, but also gives the students a hint by saying the first letter of the answer. For example: "A city in Israel that begins with Nun," or "It comes from the sky and begins with the letter Gimel" etc.

Game no. 34
Animal Or Object?

Objective:	To practice Hebrew vocabulary
Suitable for Grades:	3rd – 8th
Playing Time:	10 - 15 minutes
Materials:	None
Grouping/Organization:	Large group

Helpful Hints:

This is a challenging game.

How to Play:

One student starts by reciting the alphabet until another volunteer says "stop." The teacher makes a table on the board with columns and categories for:

- animals
- flowers/trees
- objects
- cities
- countries
- boys' names
- girls' names
- professions
- food... and so on

When the volunteer says "stop," the person who is reciting the alphabet has to stop and announce to the class what letter he is on. The students fill out the table on the board with words that match a category and begin with this letter. For example: if the letter is Aleph, for country it will be Australia, for city: AILAT (Eilat); for animal: ARYE (lion); and so on. "Older" students can try to fill out the categories in groups and earn points.

Game no. 35
Make It A Category

Objective:	To practice basic Hebrew vocabulary
Suitable for Grades:	K – 3rd
Playing Time:	5 – 10 Minutes
Materials:	A ball
Grouping/Organization:	Large group
Variations:	To make the game more challenging ask the students not to repeat the same thing that someone else had already said.

Helpful Hints:
This game is fun for reviewing vocabulary while moving around.

How to Play:
The teacher throws the ball to a student and says a category in Hebrew, for example: holidays, colors, animals, etc. The student who catches the ball has to say one word that relates to this category, for example: Shofar for holiday category, etc.

If the student who caught the ball is correct they get to throw the ball to another student, and so on, until the teacher changes the category. If the student who caught the ball gets confused they must step back from the circle.

Game no. 36
So Said The King - Verbs

Objective:	To practice Hebrew verbs
Suitable for Grades:	3rd – 6th
Playing Time:	5 – 10 Minutes
Materials:	None
Grouping/Organization:	Large group

Helpful Hints:

Make it simple for 3rd graders but challenging for 6th graders.

How to Play:

Pick a volunteer to be the king. The king says verbs in Hebrew and all the students need to obey. The volunteer needs to use verbs such as: to eat, to drink, to stand up, to sit down, to think, to read, to write, etc. The students need to follow the king's directions only if the king says: HAMELECH AMAR (המלך אמר), (the king said).

Students who act out something if the "king" did not say HAMELECH AMAR need to leave the game or sit out for 2 minutes. For verbs that cannot be acted out, the students need to pretend to obey such as: pretend to eat, pretend to think, etc.

101 - Let's have fun Roni Rosenthal-Gazit

Game no. 37
What's The Common Denominator?

Objective:	To practice family words in Hebrew
Suitable for Grades:	3rd – 6th
Playing Time:	5 – 10 Minutes
Materials:	None
Grouping/Organization:	3 – 4 Small groups

Helpful Hints:
Make it simple for 3rd graders by picking only the simplest categories. Challenge the 6th graders.

How to Play:
There are 2 ways to play this game.

Option 1: Give each group a different "family of words", for example: furniture, vegetables, means of transportation etc. Ask the students to make up words, as much as possible, that belong to this category.

Option 2: Ask each group to pick up 2 things they see in class, for example: chairs and desks. Ask them to write those objects on a piece of paper. Switch the papers between the groups, now ask the groups to figure out the family of words those items belong to.

Game no. 38
Details, More Details

Objective:	To practice Hebrew vocabulary
Suitable for Grades:	3rd- 6th
Playing Time:	5 – 10 Minutes
Materials:	Pictures with plenty of detail
Grouping/Organization:	3 -4 small groups

Helpful Hints:

The use of dictionaries is highly recommended for this game.

How to Play:

Divide the class into 3 or 4 groups. Give each group a picture that has a lot of details, for example: a picture of a farm, a supermarket, and so on. Ask each group to write down as many items as possible they see in the picture. When they are done, ask the students to sort the words into alphabetical order.

Give 1 point to the group that found at least 10 items, 2 points to the group that found over 20 items, and so on.

Game no. 39
Use Your 5 Senses

Objective:	To practice Hebrew vocabulary
Suitable for Grades:	K – 6th
Playing Time:	5 – 10 Minutes
Materials:	Paper and pencils
Grouping/Organization:	Large group

Helpful Hints:
This is a great game to play in the fall.

How to Play:
Take the students out to a field. Each student should have a piece of paper and a pencil. Ask the students to write down (without talking or sharing ideas yet) everything they can hear, see, smell, taste, or touch in the field. When you go back to the class, ask the students to share their ideas.

Younger students can add a picture next to the object. Older students can use the words to make it into a creative writing essay.

Game no. 40
Imagine That

Objective:	To practice Hebrew writing
Suitable for Grades:	3rd – 6th
Playing Time:	10 – 15 Minutes
Materials:	Paper and pencils
Grouping/Organization:	Large group

Helpful Hints:
This is a great activity for the end of the week.

How to Play:
Ask the students to lay down on the floor or carpet and close their eyes.

Start reading or telling them a story in Hebrew. Stop telling the story in the middle. Now, ask the students to go back to their desk and try to describe this story by using their five senses. Good topics for this kind of story are, for example, Shabbat Dinner, a visit to the synagogue, or a visit to a friend's house, etc.

Game no. 41
We Are Going On A Trip

Objective:	To practice conversational Hebrew and basic sentences
Suitable for Grades:	3rd – 6th
Playing Time:	7 – 10 Minutes
Materials:	None
Grouping/Organization:	Large group

Helpful Hints:

This is a great game for practicing non-complex sentences.

How to Play:

Pick a "volunteer" and send them out for 2 minutes. The teacher, or a volunteer, decides who is going on a trip, choosing all but 3-4 specific students. When the "volunteer" comes back he will ask each student "What are you bringing on the trip?"

Each student says a sentence that makes sense, but the 3-4 students who are not going on a trip say a sentence that does not make sense. For example: The first student might say: "I'm going on the trip and I'm bringing food," the second student might say: "I'm going on a trip and I'm bringing a rope." The third student, who is not going on the trip might say: "I'm going on the trip and I'm bringing a flower".

Challenge the students not to repeat the same answers that someone has already said.

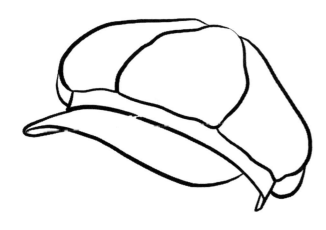

Game no. 42
What's Behind My Back?

Objective:	To practice Hebrew vocabulary
Suitable for Grades:	K - 3rd
Playing Time:	5 – 10 Minutes
Materials:	Different small items
Grouping/Organization:	Large group

Helpful Hints:

Over time you can build up a collection of interesting, small items from around the house that might be of interest to children, such as erasers, chocolate coins, keys, small toys, and so on. Be creative and try to find things that are common items but not necessarily found in the classroom. This will help children build a broader vocabulary.

How to Play:

The students sit down in a circle with their hands behind their backs and their eyes closed. Place a small item in the hands of the first student and ask them to pass it on to the student sitting next to them. You can pick either direction, left or right. Students should pass the items behind their backs to the person sitting next to them. Before you begin the game, you might want to run through the game with eyes open so the children understand which way they are going to pass the objects.

While playing the game, students should pass the items while keeping their eyes closed.

When the teacher claps their hands, everybody opens their eyes. The student holding the item should try to guess what it is. No-one else is allowed to guess at this point. If the student holding the item cannot guess the item they can choose from the following options:

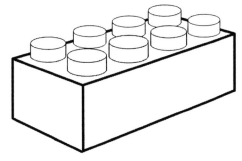

1. Ask one friend to help them guess what the item is.

2. The student who is trying to guess can ask for help from the rest of the class by asking them to choose between two possibilities. Students vote on their choice by raising their hands. For example, the student might say: "If you think it's an eraser, please raise your hand." And then, "If you think it's a tape, please raise your hand." The student then has to choose which item they are going to guess, based on the response from classmates.

The student holding the item makes a guess at what the item is. The teacher can decide between allowing students to keep the items they guess correctly or assigning points to the student and the one with the most points wins.

Game no. 43
Say It Again Please

Objective:	To practice Hebrew sentences
Suitable for Grades:	K – 1st
Playing Time:	7 – 10 Minutes
Materials:	None
Grouping/Organization:	Pairs

Helpful Hints:
This is a very funny game.

How to Play:
Divide the class into pairs. Give each pair one sentence. The first student calls out the sentence and keeps repeating it over and over without getting confused or starting to laugh. The other student in the pair tries to get the first student confused or laughing by making silly faces. Once the student gets confused or starts laughing they switch roles.

You can keep changing the sentences or ask the students to come up with their own sentences.

Game no. 44
So What's the Sentence? – Advanced Game

Objective:	To practice Hebrew sentences
Suitable for Grades:	3rd – 6th
Playing Time:	10 – 15 Minutes
Materials:	One long sentence printed on a card and cut into words
Grouping/Organization:	Large group

Helpful Hints:

This is a great game for practicing phrases and word order in sentences.

How to Play:

Print or write one long sentence on a piece of cardboard. Cut the cardboard into smaller cards so that there is only one word on each card. Now, mix up the cards and give the cards to the students. Ask the students to stand in a line according to the right order of the sentence or phrase, so that the student who is holding the first word of the sentence is the first in line, the student holding the next word is the second in line, and so on.

Note: Sometimes there is more than one way to put the words into a sentence.

Variations:

Option 1: Divide the class into 3-4 groups, and give a sentence to each group. The wining group is the one whose members line up first in the correct order.

Option 2: For older students you can write or print 2 or more sentences and cut them into cards with words. The students need to figure out the original sentences first.

Game no. 45
I Spy

Objective:	To practice basic Hebrew vocabulary and conversational skills
Suitable for Grades:	K – 3rd
Playing Time:	5 – 10 Minutes
Materials:	None
Grouping/Organization:	Large group
Variations:	Students can also pick a friend in class to practice body parts. For example: "I spy a boy with yellow hair and brown eyes."

Helpful Hints:

This is a nice game to play in the morning or as a review of basic vocabulary of shapes, colors, and items in the classroom.

How to Play:

Students sit in a circle and look around them. One student volunteers to describe an object they can see, for example: "It's yellow and is shaped like a circle ..."
The other students guess the object.

Game no. 46
What's The Question?

Objective:	To practice asking questions and giving answers
Suitable for Grades:	2nd – 4th
Playing Time:	5 – 10 Minutes
Materials:	None
Grouping/Organization:	Pairs or large group

איזו חיה אתה הכי אוהב?

Helpful Hints:
This is a nice game for practicing question words in Hebrew.

How to Play:
There are 2 ways to play this game:

Option 1: Divide the class into pairs. Each student has to write on a piece of paper 3 sets of questions. When the time is up, the students exchange papers and write down their answers.

מה האות הראשונה במילה "שבת"?

Option 2: Each student writes one question on a piece of paper, and folds the paper. All the students sit in a circle and put all the folded papers in the center in a pile. Each student takes a turn to take one note from the pile and answer the question.

מה האות השלישית בא'-ב'?

כמה חיות באו לתיבה של נח?

Game no. 47
The Spokesmen

Objective:	To practice question decoding in Hebrew
Suitable for Grades:	K – 6th
Playing Time:	5 – 10 minutes
Materials:	A Hebrew story or text
Grouping/Organization:	Large group
Variations:	See below.

Helpful Hints:
This is a fun game and good for moving around in class.

How to Play:
The teacher or a volunteer is called «The spokesman. The spokesman reads a story or text in Hebrew. Every time the spokesman reads a special word (which the class agrees on beforehand), all the students jump out of their seats and quickly sit down again. For example: every time the spokesman says the word «HAYOM» (היום) (today), everybody jumps out of their seats.

A variation: For younger students, instead of using a word, you can use a vowel with a letter, for example: BET with KAMATS (בָ), Bet with SEGOL (בֶ), or VET with HIRIK (בִ), or the sound VE (וְ) that stands for the word: AND.

Game no. 48
Opposites

Objective:	To practice Hebrew vocabulary
Suitable for Grades:	K – 6th
Playing Time:	5 – 10 Minutes
Materials:	A ball for each pair
Grouping/Organization:	Pairs/large group

Helpful Hints:
This is a fun game for review.

How to Play:
There are 2 ways to play this game:

Option 1: The teacher divides the class into pairs. Each pair gets a ball. The pairs throw the ball from one student to the other. The person throwing the ball says a word and the person catching it has to say the opposite word. The winning pair is the one that finds the most opposite words.

Option 2: The teacher throws the ball and says a word. The student who catches the ball has to say the opposite word. A student who forgets or gets confused has to sit out.

Game no. 49
Tic Tac Toe

Objective:	To practice Hebrew vocabulary or trivia questions
Suitable for Grades:	K – 6th (simple words for younger students, more complex words for older students)
Playing Time:	5 – 10 Minutes
Materials:	None
Grouping/Organization:	2 groups

Helpful Hints:
This is a fun game for review.

How to Play:
Divide the class into 2 groups. Ask each group a question. The questions can be things such as, "How do you say in Hebrew", "What is the opposite of…", "What's the meaning of…", etc.

Make a chart on the board. When a group answers correctly they choose where to place an "X" or an "O" on the chart. The winning group is the one who fills out all X's or O's in a row.

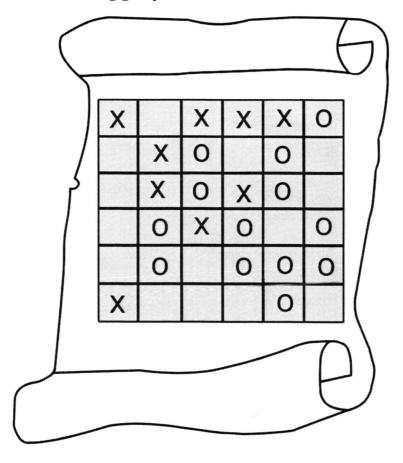

Game no. 50
Match All Four

Objective:	To practice family words in Hebrew
Suitable for Grades:	K – 3rd
Playing Time:	5 – 10 Minutes
Materials:	Flash cards
Grouping/Organization:	3 – 4 Groups

Helpful Hints:

This game works best if there are no more than 4 students in a group.

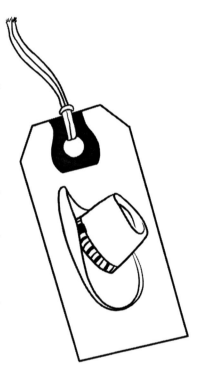

How to Play:

Divide the class into small groups, with no more than 4 students in a group. Use 16 flash cards for each group. You can use the same flash cards for all the groups. On the desk place 4 titles: types of food, animals, holidays, and clothes, for example. Give each student only 2 cards. The player whose turn it is to choose, picks one student in their group and asks for their cards of the same set. For example, "Do you have anything that has to do with food?" The students can only ask for sets if they are holding at least one card from this category.

When a student is called upon, if he/she has a card that fits the description, he/she has to give his/her card to the person who asked for it. If he/she does not have a card, the person who is asking draws a card from the deck. The turn then passes on to the player who was asked.

When a student manages to collect all 4 cards belonging to the same set, they place them down on the "title" card.

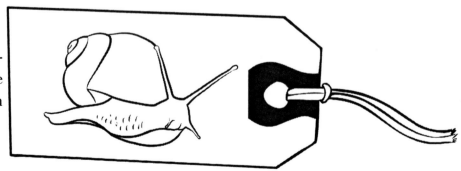

Game no. 51
Are You Brave?

Objective:	To practice Hebrew comprehension
Suitable for Grades:	K - 3rd
Playing Time:	5 – 10 Minutes
Materials:	Cards with assignments
Grouping/Organization:	Large group

Helpful Hints:

This is a very funny game to play that gets the students to move around.

How to Play:

Give the students cards and ask them to write down 2-3 assignments (in Hebrew) for their friends. (Teachers - please go over the cards before you start playing and make sure the assignments are reasonable and make sense).

Ask the students to sit down in a circle, and put all the cards in a pile in the center. Each student takes a turn and pulls out one card. The student reads the assignment on the card, tries to understand the task, and carries it out. Students who understand and carry out the assignment successfully get 1 point. The winner is the student with the most points. Students who get confused, or do not understand the assignments, skip a turn.

קפוץ הכי גבוה שאתה יכול

Game no. 52
Question Bingo

Objective:	To practice Hebrew comprehension
Suitable for Grades:	K – 6th
Playing Time:	10 Minutes
Materials:	Bingo cards with printed answers
Grouping/Organization:	Large group

Helpful Hints:

This game is fun for learning Hebrew questions and vocabulary related to the holidays.

How to Play:

The teacher gives each student a chart with 16 words filled in. These words serve as answers to questions. The answers to all possible questions should also be printed on paper as reference, but only sixteen of them are used on the chart (like a Bingo chart).

The teacher then asks questions. Students need to identify the correct answer to the question and if the answer is on their chart, they put an X over it. When a student fills out a line of words (answers), or a diagonal line they shout "BINGO."

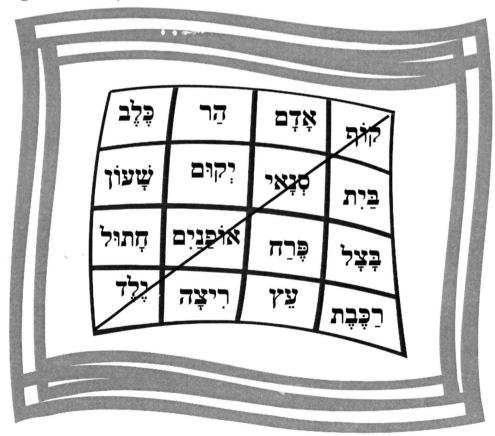

Game no. 53
What Happened First?

Objective:	To practice reading sentences and understanding them in Hebrew.
Suitable for Grades:	K – 2nd
Playing Time:	10 Minutes
Materials:	4 sentences on 4 cards
Grouping/Organization:	3 - 4 groups

Helpful Hints:

This is a good logic game for learning basic sentences.

How to Play:

Divide the class into 3-4 groups. Each group gets 4 sentences written on 4 different cards. The cards should be written like a story: for example: "He woke up in the morning. He got dressed. He washed his face. He ate breakfast and went to school." When you have written the sentences, mix up the cards so that the sentences are not in the right order. You can add a picture on each card to help the kids understand what is happening in the story. The students must put the sentences in order. On the other side of the cards you can print out a phrase or letters from a word, such that if the students arrange the cards in the right order, they will get a phrase or a word of encouragement (Such as: "Good job, you did it") on the other side. For older students you can use a longer story with more than 4 sentences.

Game no. 54
Word Dominoes

Objective:	To practice reading and understanding basic vocabulary or family words
Suitable for Grades:	3rd – 6th
Playing Time:	5 – 10 Minutes
Materials:	Domino cards
Grouping/Organization:	3 – 4 small groups
Variations:	The Dominos cards can match pictures and words, questions and answers, or family words.

Helpful Hints:

This is a nice, relaxing game. No more than 5 students in a group.

How to Play:

Divide the students into groups of five. Give two domino cards to each student in the group. Put any remaining cards in a pile in the center. The players must not show their cards to each other. The first player puts one of his cards in the center of the circle. It can be a card with a word or a picture. The next player tries to match a picture to the word, or word to the picture, and puts his card down. If the second player does not have a matching word or picture, then this player draws a card from the pile and the next player takes a turn.

The game continues until none of the players can match a word or picture and there are no more cards in the pile. The winner is the first student who gets rid of their cards.

101 - Let's have fun Roni Rosenthal-Gazit

Game no. 55
Crossword Puzzles

Objective:	To practice basic vocabulary or family words
Suitable for Grades:	3rd – 6th
Playing Time:	10 Minutes
Materials:	Cards
Grouping/Organization:	Pairs or individually

Helpful Hints:
This is a nice, relaxing game. No more than 2 students in a group.

How to Play:
Crossword puzzles are always a nice activity at the end of a lesson. They are a great way to review basic words in Hebrew, or vocabulary for the holidays.

There are some websites where you can type in the words in Hebrew and they will make crossword puzzles ready to be printed.

הגדרות

מאוזן ⟷

1. נושבת בחורף
3. תולים עליו בגדים ומעילים.
4. «_____ ולבשמים נפשי מיחלה» שיר של הבדלה.
6. שם של ספור ילדים ידוע: «_____ והחיה»
8. מילה נרדפת לנודד, מטייל.
9. אחד התווים במוסיקה.
10. שם של צבע.
11. הספר הכי חשוב ליהודים.

מאונך ⇓

2. עונה בשנה.
4. כשנפרדים מחבר אומרים: «...........»
5. מילה נרדפת לדף (עם יוד אחת).
7. לא אתמול ולא מחר אלא _____.
9. הדוור מביא לוו כל יום

Some good websites are:

http://www.crossword.co.il/

http:// www.edu-negev.gov.il/

Game no. 56
Yes/No Flags

Objective:	To practice Hebrew vocabulary or questions that have a "yes" or "no" answer
Suitable for Grades:	K - 3rd
Playing Time:	10 Minutes
Materials:	Yes flag, No flag
Grouping/Organization:	Large group or pairs
Variations:	See below

Helpful Hints:

This game is nice and easy. Have the kids make their own flags.

How to Play:

Before starting the game, give the students 2 blank pieces of paper and crayons. On one piece of paper they have to write KEN (כן) (yes), and draw pictures of things that are positive for them (things they like about Hebrew). On the other piece they write LO (לא) (no) and draw things they don't like.

For the game: The teacher asks a question. If the answer is yes, students lift up the "yes" flag, if the answer is no students lift the "no" flag. Questions could be things like: "is SHULCHAN (שולחן) the right word for a chair?" etc.

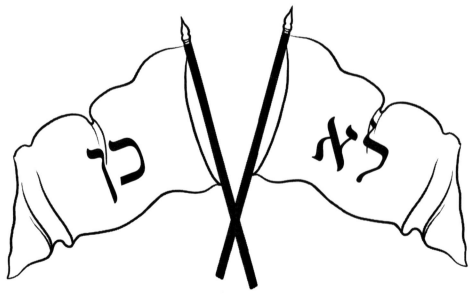

Variations:

You can divide the class into pairs. One student holds the "yes" flag, the other holds the "no" flag. Alternatively, instead of using flags, you can just have students stand up if they think the answer is yes, and sit down if they think the answer is no.

Game no. 57
Who Am I?

Objective:	To practice Hebrew vocabulary
Suitable for Grades:	3rd – 8th
Playing Time:	10 Minutes
Materials:	Flash cards with pictures
Grouping/Organization:	Large group
Variations:	For older students: tape character cards on each student's back. Each student tries to find out what character they have on their back.

Helpful Hints:

This is a nice game. Don't use more than 4-5 cards and don't play for more than 10 minutes.

How to Play:

Pick a volunteer. Tape a card with a character/image to their back so that all the students except the volunteer can see the character. The volunteer proceeds to ask questions and guesses the character on their back. Students can answer using full sentences (more than yes or no,) but without giving away the answer. Students can also give the volunteer up to 3 hints. Examples of characters are: a clown, a soldier, a famous singer, the president, etc.

Game no. 58
A Ball To The Sky

Objective:	To practice answering questions in Hebrew
Suitable for Grades:	K – 4th
Playing Time:	10 Minutes
Materials:	A ball
Grouping/Organization:	Large group

Helpful Hints:
It is better to play this game outside in a field or an open area.

How to Play:
One student stands in the middle of the circle and holds a ball. The student holding the ball asks a question in Hebrew. Once they have asked the question, they throw the ball into the air and say KADUR LASHAMAIM (כדור לשמים), (a ball to the sky). If a student knows the answer to the question they try to catch the ball. If the student who catches the ball answers correctly, they get to stand in the middle and ask another question while throwing the ball to the sky. If they do not answer correctly, they return to their position and the student who asked the question continues playing in the middle of the circle.

101 - Let's have fun   Roni Rosenthal-Gazit

Game no. 59
The Phone Is Broken

Objective:	To practice Hebrew vocabulary
Suitable for Grades:	3rd – 6th
Playing Time:	5 – 7 Minutes
Materials:	None
Grouping/Organization:	Large group

Helpful Hints:

You can play this game a couple of times. Just switch the first word.

How to Play:

Everybody sits in a circle. The first student says a word. The student sitting next to him repeats the first word and adds another word to form a sentence. The third student repeats the first and second words and adds another word to the sentence, and so on. The last student has to remember all the words in the sentence and add a word of his own. The sentence might turn out to be funny, but it should make sense.

Game no. 60
My Name Is... And I Am A...

Objective:	To practice Hebrew vocabulary
Suitable for Grades:	K – 1st
Playing Time:	5 – 7 Minutes
Materials:	None
Grouping/Organization:	Large group
Variations:	See below

Helpful Hints:

You can take a couple of turns with this game. Just ask the students to choose a different item, animal, or object each time they choose. This game can be played at the beginning of the year or as an introductory game.

How to Play:

Everybody sits in a circle. Each student says their name and then adds the name of an object that starts with the first letter of their name. For example: My name is Roni and I am RAKEVET (רכבת), (a train). Older students can also try to explain the connection between their name and the object. For example: I'm RAKEVET, because I'm always in a hurry.

Variations:

The Second student repeats the first name and object, and then adds their own name and object, and so on. For example: He is Moshe MATATE (מטאטא), (broom), and I am David and DAG (דג) (fish).

Game no. 61
Treasure Hunt

Objective:	To practice Hebrew vocabulary
Suitable for Grades:	3rd – 6th
Playing Time:	15 - 20 Minutes
Materials:	Needs preparation time, paper and envelopes
Grouping/Organization;	3–4 small groups, no more than 5 students in a group
Variations:	See below

Helpful Hints:
Try to keep the game moving.

How to Play:
Hide 5-6 objects in the class or in a field, and attach an envelope to each one of the hidden objects. The objects should not be too big for the students to move or carry, and they should not be hidden in places that are too easy to find.

Tape an envelope on the hidden object that includes a clue (in Hebrew) for how to find the next object. Do not make the clues too easy or the game will be over too fast. For example: "It's white and black and always moving as if it's running somewhere" (Answer: the clock in the classroom). Behind the clock you can tape the envelope with the clue to the next object. When a group finds an envelope, they must put it back in the same place for the next group to find, or else make more than one envelope so each group can take one. Start the game by giving students the first clue in an envelope.

Variations:
You can time the students and the winner is the first group who solves all the clues and get back first. You can make different clues for each group and see where they end up. You should stagger start times for the groups by a couple of minutes from one another, so they will not be able to reveal the clues before the next group reaches that target.

Game no. 62
Step On It

Objective:	To practice Hebrew vocabulary for the holidays
Suitable for Grades:	K – 6th
Playing Time:	10 Minutes
Materials:	Flash cards with pictures of symbols
Grouping/Organization:	Large group

Helpful Hints:

This game is a winner for the holidays.

How to Play:

Print out, or draw pictures, with symbols of the holidays and the vocabulary you are teaching in class. Each card should be on a full page (8.5 x 11) and preferably laminated. Spread out the cards on the floor. Ask the students to start walking around, without stepping on the pictures. It is nice to play music while the students are walking.

When the teacher claps their hands or stops the music, the students stop and step on the nearest card lying on the floor (like musical chairs). The teacher will then call a symbol and the student standing on that symbol must give back the card and go back to their seat. For example: if the cards are for the Tishrei Holidays, the teacher might call: "The student who is standing on a symbol of Shoffar must give back the card and go back to their seat."

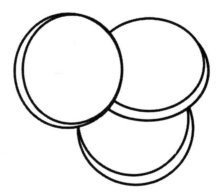

For younger students only the word of the symbols should appear on the card. For older students you can add a couple of sentences about the meaning of the symbol and ask the student to read the paragraph out loud before they go back to their seat.

Game no. 63
If It Wasn't A Chair, It Would Be A...

Objective:	To practice conversational Hebrew
Suitable for Grades:	3rd – 6th
Playing Time:	5 – 10 Minutes
Materials:	None
Grouping/Organization:	Large group

Helpful Hints:

This is a very creative game. Kids just love it!

How to Play:

The students sit in a circle. Each student picks an object in class and says: "If it wasn't an X, it would be a ..." and then they complete the sentence using their imagination. Older students can explain why this object reminds them of something else. Examples of objects are chairs, tables, pictures, the board, etc. Students who get the most creative ideas and explanations win points or prizes. You will be surprised how imaginative children can be in their ideas and their creativity. A chair can quickly become a horse in the vivid imagination of children.

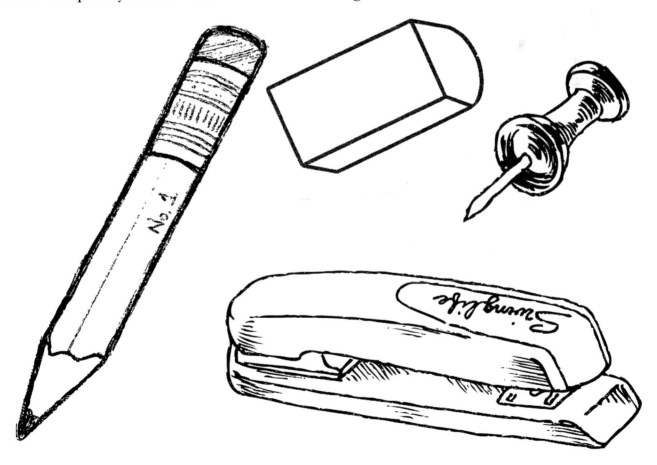

Game no. 64
Be Creative

Objective:	To practice Hebrew sentences
Suitable for Grades:	K - 3rd
Playing Time:	5 – 10 Minutes
Materials:	Pictures of various objects
Grouping/Organization:	Large group

Helpful Hints:

This is a very creative game and very funny.

How to Play:

The students sit in a circle. Each student gets 2 different pictures that are not related in any way. The students must use both pictures in a sentence. For example: if one student gets a picture of a table and a picture of a cat, the student might say: "Yesterday, I saw a table in class, after a second it started meowing like a cat". Most of the sentences are so silly the kids just can't stop laughing.

Game no. 65
From Letters Into Words

Objective:	To practice basic vocabulary and communication skills
Suitable for Grades:	K - 3rd
Playing Time:	5 – 10 Minutes
Materials:	Flash cards with letters of the alphabet
Grouping/Organization:	Individuals or pairs

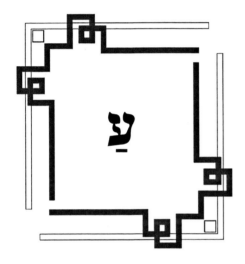

Helpful Hints:
Keep the negotiation simple and friendly.

How to Play:
Each student gets 5 cards with letters of the Alphabet on them. The object of the game is to make a word out of those letters. However, each student also needs to pair up with a friend and negotiate with them to swap letters. The negotiation must be in Hebrew. You can also let students work in pairs, but this time they have to come up with 2 words by pooling all the letters. Students are not allowed to see each other's cards before deciding if they want to pair up, and once they pair with someone, they cannot reverse their decision.

The negotiation must be valuable to both students so they can exchange one card for one or two cards, but no more.

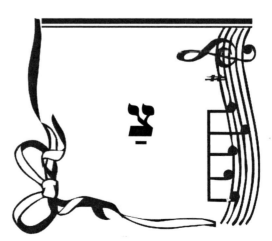

Game no. 66
Mom Went To Market

Objective:	To practice basic vocabulary
Suitable for Grades:	K - 3rd
Playing Time:	5 – 10 Minutes
Materials:	Flash cards with items you find in the supermarket
Grouping/Organization:	Large group

Helpful Hints:

This game gives a nice review of food and grocery vocabulary.

How to Play:

The students sit in a circle. The cards are placed in a pile in the middle of the circle. The first student picks up the top card and puts it face up in front of him and says: "Mom went to the supermarket and bought…." The student names the item in the picture. The next student picks up the next card from the pile and says: "Mom went to the supermarket and bought…". This student repeats the first item and the item on their own card. The third student repeats the first and second items and adds the next item, and so on. By the time it gets to the last student, the sentence has become very long! Items can be fruits, vegetables, meat, fish, soap, etc.

Game no. 67
Crossword Puzzle – Make It Yourself

Objective:	To practice basic vocabulary
Suitable for Grades:	3rd – 8th
Playing Time:	15 – 20 Minutes
Materials:	Paper with 10 x 10 grids (20 squares)
Grouping/Organization:	Large group

Helpful Hints:
A challenging game.

How to Play:
Each student gets a blank piece of paper with a table made up of 20 squares. Students fill in 7 or 8 words to create a crossword puzzle. The students come up with the words by themselves so that the words will be different from one puzzle to the next. Students can leave some squares blank or fill them in with extra letters. When they have finished making the crossword puzzle they switch puzzles with their friends.

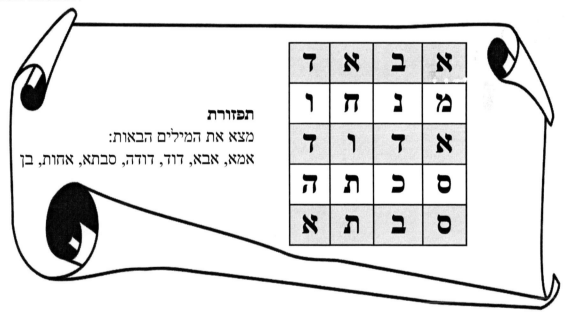

תפזורת
מצא את המילים הבאות:
אמא, אבא, דוד, דודה, סבתא, אחות, בן

Students have to try and find the words hiding in the puzzle which their friends have made up for them.

Game no. 68
How Do They Say It In Gematria?

Objective:	To practice Hebrew words, sentences and phrases
Suitable for Grades:	3rd – 8th
Playing Time:	5 – 10 Minutes
Materials:	Paper
Grouping/Organization:	Individuals/pairs
Variations:	The teacher can split the class into small groups when each group needs to hide words behind numbers. When they switch papers, students attempt to figure out what phrase or sentence is hiding.

Helpful Hints:

A mathematical way to practice Hebrew.

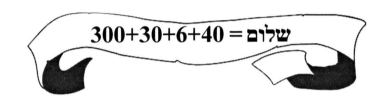

300+30+6+40 = שלום

How to Play:

Gematria is a nice way of assigning numbers to the letters of the alphabet. In Gematria each letter translates to a number. There are a couple of ways to play games in Gematria. The teacher can write a phrase, sentence, or words on the board and ask the students to translate it into numbers. Another way to play is for the teacher to hide words or phrases behind the numbers and ask students to find what words are hiding there. For example the number: 300+30+6+40 equals the word SHALOM (שלום) in Hebrew.

Attached is a table:

Points	Hebrew Letters	Points	Hebrew Letters
1	Aleph	30	Lamed
2	Bet	40	Mem
3	Gimel	50	Nun
4	Daled	60	Samekh
5	He	70	Ayin
6	Vav	80	Pe
7	Zayin	90	Tsadi
8	Heth	100	Qoph
9	Teth	200	Resh
10	Yod	300	Shin
11	Kaph	400	Tav

Game no. 69
I say...

Objective:	To practice conversational Hebrew
Suitable for Grades:	3rd – 6th
Playing Time:	5 – 10 Minutes
Materials:	None
Grouping/Organization:	Pairs
Variations:	See below

Helpful Hints:

This game can be played in writing.

How to Play:

Divide the class into groups of pairs. One student starts a sentence and the other one has to finish it. For example: one student might say: "Yesterday, when I was walking in the street" The other student could then add: "I saw a red car waving at me". Older students can keep on switching turns and make it into a story.

Variations:

You can play this game in writing, where the first student writes down the beginning of the sentence and their friend has to finish the sentence.

Another option is to ask the students to sit in a circle and the first student begins a story. Each student adds another sentence to the story.

Game no. 70
Cut It Out

Objective:	To practice Hebrew vocabulary
Suitable for Grades:	K - 3rd
Playing Time:	10 – 15 Minutes
Materials:	Hebrew newspapers, scissors, glue and paper
Grouping/Organization:	3 - 4 groups
Variations:	Older students can also cut out words from the newspaper and make them into sentences.

Helpful Hints:

Great for practicing letters.

How to Play:

Divide the class into 3-4 groups. Each group gets some old newspapers in Hebrew, scissors, glue, and a blank piece of paper. The teacher assigns the group a letter of the Alphabet. Each group has to cut out at least 5 words that begin with the assigned letter.

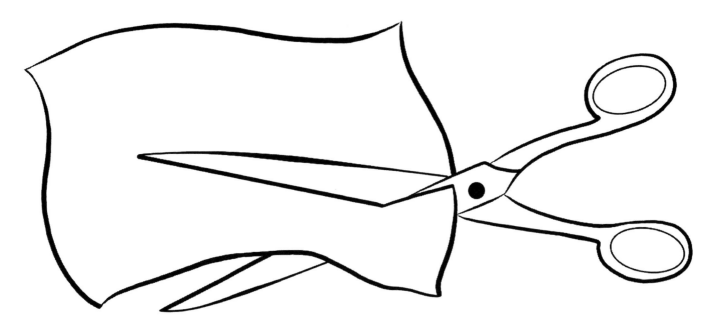

The teacher can decide to give each group more than one letter, or conjunctions, pronouns, or other common words like VEGAM (וגם) (and), HEM (הם) (they), etc.

Game no. 71
The Spokesman And The Pantomime

Objective:	To practice Hebrew comprehension
Suitable for Grades:	3rd – 8th
Playing Time:	10 -15 Minutes
Materials:	A story or text in Hebrew
Grouping/Organization:	Pairs

Helpful Hints:

This is a very funny game, the kids just love it!

How to Play:

One student volunteers to tell or read a story to the class, and another volunteers to be the pantomime. While the first student is telling the story, the pantomime acts it out. The pantomime uses his hands and body to act out what is being related. This game usually turns out to be very funny. Students love participating in the game and enjoy the stories.

Game no. 72
Catch The Balloon

Objective: To practice reading letters, words, sentences and phrases

Suitable for Grades: K – 8th
Playing Time: 10 Minutes
Materials: Balloons
Grouping/Organization: Individuals
Variations: Write a sentence or a phrase on the balloons and ask the students to place the balloons in order. Or simply write the last word of a sentence on the balloon and ask students to find the balloon that has a matching word for the logical end of the sentence.

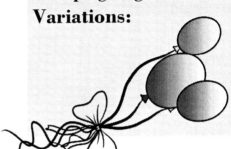

Helpful Hints:
This is a very popular game. It's great for moving around.

How to Play:
The teacher or volunteers write letters or words on balloons. The teacher blows up the balloons and spreads them around in the classroom. The teacher, or a volunteer, then calls out a letter or a word, and the students run between the balloons attempting to find the one with the letter or word written on it.

The teacher can decide whether to let the winner pop the balloon, keep it, or give it back.

Game no. 73
Anyone For Spelling?

Objective:	To practice reading, comprehension and decoding
Suitable for Grades:	3rd – 8th
Playing Time:	5 – 10 Minutes
Materials:	Sentences or short story
Grouping/Organization:	3 – 4 small groups

Helpful Hints:

Great game for reading practice.

How to Play:

Divide the class into 3-4 small groups. Each group gets a sentence or a short story with missing or misspelled words. The group tries to figure out which words are missing or misspelled.

Another way to play this game is to ask each group to write a misspelled story for the other group. Swap stories between the groups, so that each group has to figure out the misspelled words the other group made for them and then correct them.

Game no. 74
It's Trivia Time

Objective:	To practice Hebrew vocabulary
Suitable for Grades:	3rd – 8th
Playing Time:	10 - 15 Minutes
Materials:	Flash cards with questions in envelopes
Grouping/Organization:	2 Groups

Helpful Hints:

This is a great game for reviewing holiday vocabulary.

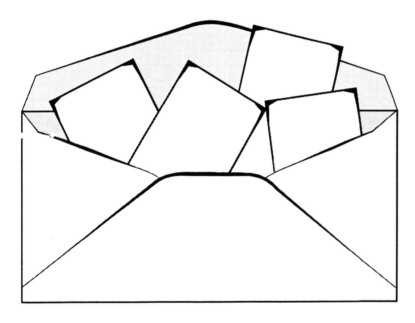

How to Play:

The teacher divides the class into 2 groups. Choose boys versus girls, groups divided by last names, or divide the class in the way you prefer. Each group has to send a representative to answer one question. The representative who is first to provide the correct answer gets to draw an envelope for his group. The envelopes contain questions like "How do you say... in Hebrew". You can include questions about anything, including holiday symbols and their meaning, or any other subject area.

Each envelope is weighted with a different number of points according to the level of difficulty of the question. The group earns points if they know the right answer. If the first group doesn't know the answer, the second group gets a chance to answer the question and earn the points. The group that earns the most points wins.

Game no. 75
The Survey

Objective:	To practice conversational Hebrew
Suitable for Grades:	3rd – 8th
Playing Time:	10 Minutes
Materials:	None, although optional hats and costumes could be used
Grouping/Organization:	Large group

Helpful Hints:

This is a very funny game for practicing Hebrew.

How to Play:

The teacher suggests a topic for discussion or an opening sentence to the class. Two volunteers are the interviewers and the other students in class are the "people walking in the street". The interviewers take turns to ask "the people" questions regarding a topic or begin an interview with an opening sentence. The people in the street reply and give their opinion.

A great way to get kids involved in this game is to supply costumes, or even just hats, for the people in the street. This way they can try being different people and answer the questions differently according to the role they are playing. For example, a student wearing a clown hat or clown costume can respond like a clown, etc.

Game no. 76
Ahhhh!

Objective:	To learn and practice new Hebrew vocabulary
Suitable for Grades:	K - 3rd
Playing Time:	5 – 10 Minutes
Materials:	None
Grouping/Organization:	Large group

סַרְטָן הַגְּהָרוֹת

Helpful Hints:
A fun game but it can get very loud.

How to Play:
Everyone sits in a circle. One volunteer leaves the room. While they are out, the group decides on a word. It can be a new word that the teacher teaches the class for the first time. When the volunteer comes back, everybody shouts the word together. The volunteer has to guess what the word means. He can ask the class to shout it again up to 5 times. If the volunteer is right, he gets 1 point, but if he is not, pick another volunteer and another word, and start the game all over again.

Game no. 77
An Impossible Dialog

Objective:	To practice conversational Hebrew
Suitable for Grades:	3rd – 6th
Playing Time:	10 Minutes
Materials:	None
Grouping/Organization:	Large group

Helpful Hints:

A very funny game.

How to Play:

Everybody sits in a circle. The first student asks the student sitting next to them a question. The second student takes the last two words from the first student's question, and makes it into a new question. The second student asks the third student the new question and so on. For example: The first student might ask: "Where were you yesterday?" The second student might turn that into: "Were you at the Bank yesterday?" The third student could then ask: "Was the Bank closed yesterday?" And so on...

Game no. 78
The Artist – Words, Sentences and Phrases

Objective:	To practice vocabulary, phrases, sentences and more
Suitable for Grades:	K – 6th
Playing Time:	5 – 10 Minutes
Materials:	Flash cards with Hebrew words, phrases, sentences, names of the holidays or movies.
Grouping/Organization:	2 Groups

Helpful Hints:

This is a great game, and very funny.

How to Play:

The teacher divides the class into 2 groups. Choose boys versus girls, groups divided by last names, or divide the class in the way you prefer. Each group selects a representative. The representative gets a card with one word in Hebrew, a phrase, the name of a movie, the name of a holiday, and so on. Each representative gets exactly 2 minutes to draw a picture for their group. They cannot speak or write the word. They must convey what the card says only by drawing a picture. Each group guesses what their representative is drawing on the board. Limit each group to 3 guesses.

Game no. 79
Fruit Salad

Objective: To practice the names of fruit in Hebrew
Suitable for Grades: K - 3rd
Playing Time: 10 Minutes
Materials: Flash cards with pictures of fruit
Grouping/Organization: Large group

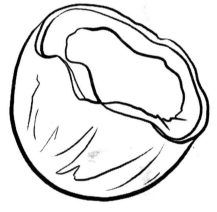

Helpful Hints:

Hang the flash cards on the board to remind the kids of the names of fruits. You can play the same game with vegetables.

How to Play:

The students sit on chairs in the circle. Each student, (including the volunteer), is assigned a name of a fruit in Hebrew, for example: Banana (בננה), apple (תפוח), grapes (ענבים), etc. One "volunteer" stands in the middle so that there is one chair missing. The volunteer announces the name of a fruit in Hebrew. The students, who were assigned this fruit, get up from their chairs to quickly find another chair and sit back down. The volunteer in the middle must also find a chair and sit down. This leaves one student standing without a chair. This is the new "volunteer". When the volunteer calls: "SALAT PEIROT" A "fruit Salad" (סלט פירות) everybody must switch chairs no matter what fruit they were assigned.

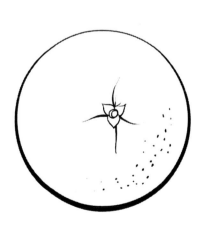

Game no. 80
A Picture Story

Objective:	To practice basic Hebrew vocabulary
Suitable for Grades:	K - 3rd
Playing Time:	10 Minutes
Materials:	Short stories and pencils
Grouping/Organization:	5 - 6 Groups

Helpful Hints:
A nice, creative game.

How to Play:
Divide the class into 5-6 groups with no more than 3 students in a group. Each group gets a story. Students cover up some words in the story with white stickers and draw pictures that represent the words. The teacher switches the papers between the groups, and each group has to write down the missing words.

בחוה של דוד משה היתה _____ , שכל היום עשתה "מו מו"

Game no. 81
Words That Begin With...

Objective:	To practice Hebrew vocabulary
Suitable for Grades:	K – 6th
Playing Time:	10 Minutes
Materials:	2 – 3 Balls, one for each group
Grouping/Organization:	2 – 3 Groups

Helpful Hints:

A fun game.

How to Play:

The teacher divides the class into 2-3 groups. Students stand in a circle in their group. The teacher gives each group a ball and a letter. The students pass the ball to one another and say words that begin with the assigned letter. The students cannot repeat a word that someone else has already said. The wining group is the one that gets the most words.

Game no. 82
No Space

Objective:	To practice reading Hebrew sentences
Suitable for Grades:	3rd – 6th
Playing Time:	10 Minutes
Materials:	Texts in Hebrew
Grouping/Organization:	3 – 4 Groups

Helpful Hints:
This is a nice game for practicing reading and decoding.

How to Play:
The teacher divides the class into 3-4 groups. Each group gets a Hebrew text, story, or sentence with no spaces between the words. Each group has to figure out where the spaces between the words are meant to be.

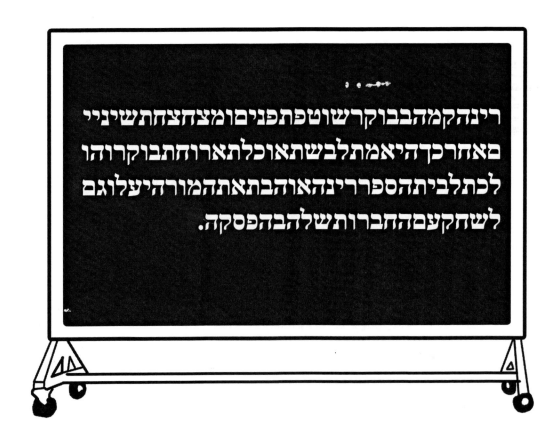

101 - Let's have fun Roni Rosenthal-Gazit

Game no. 83
Rhyming

Objective:	To practice Hebrew vocabulary
Suitable for Grades:	2nd – 6th
Playing Time:	5 – 7 Minutes
Materials:	A ball
Grouping/Organization:	Large group

Helpful Hints:
This is a great game for reviewing vocabulary.

How to Play:
The students stand in a circle. The first student throws the ball to another student in the circle and says a word. The student who catches the ball says a word that rhymes with the first word. If the catcher knows a rhyming word they say it and then make up another word and throw the ball to someone else. If the catcher cannot think up a rhyming word they throw the ball to someone else and sit out for 2 minutes before they can come back to the game.

Game no. 84
With Vowels or Without?

Objective:	To practice Hebrew vocabulary
Suitable for Grades:	6th – 8th
Playing Time:	5 Minutes
Materials:	None
Grouping/Organization:	2 Groups

Helpful Hints:

A challenging game. In this game, children will benefit from using a dictionary.

How to Play:

The teacher divides the class into 2 groups. Choose boys versus girls, groups divided by last names, or divide the class in the way you prefer. The groups brainstorm words that become new words when the vowels are changed. Each group brainstorms as many words as possible that have different meanings just by changing vowels. For example:

IM or AM (עַם או עִם) = with or nation
RECHEV or RACHAV (רֶכֶב או רָכַב) = car or ride
REVACH or RUACH (רֶוַח או רוּחַ) = space or wind

Game no. 85
Follow The Arrow

Objective:	To practice Hebrew vocabulary
Suitable for Grades:	3rd – 6th
Playing Time:	10 - 15 Minutes
Materials:	Cards with directions
Grouping/Organization:	3 – 4 Small groups

Helpful Hints:
This game needs some preparation time. It is better to play in the hallway, playground, or a field.

How to Play:
Divide the class into 3-4 groups, with no more than 4 students in a group. Hide 3-4 "treasures", one for each group in certain places. Now, give each group a collection of 5-6 cards. The cards contain directions for how to find the treasures. Each group gets directions to a different treasure.

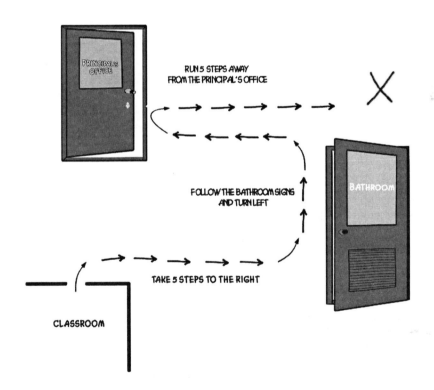

If the students follow the directions they will get to the treasure. The directions can be things like: "Take 5 steps to the right", "Follow the bathroom signs and turn left", or "Run 5 steps away from the principal's office".

Game no. 86
A Picture

Objective:	To practice Hebrew vocabulary
Suitable for Grades:	K – 1st
Playing Time:	10 Minutes
Materials:	Flash cards with pictures
Grouping/Organization:	Large group

Helpful Hints:
This game is quite basic and easy.

How to Play:
Each student gets a card with a picture on it. The teacher calls an object in Hebrew. The student, holding the card and recognizes the name of the item in Hebrew, returns the card to the teacher and gets 1 point. They can then get another card with a different picture and earn more points. The winner is the student who gets most points.

Game no. 87
One Out Of Four

Objective:	To practice general vocabulary and holiday vocabulary
Suitable for Grades:	K – 6th
Playing Time:	10 Minutes
Materials:	None
Grouping/Organization:	3 – 4 Group

Helpful Hints:

This is a nice game for review.

How to Play:

The teacher divides the class into 3-4 groups. The teacher asks each group a question and gives them 4 options from which to choose the right answer. The group that answers the question on the first guess earns 10 points. If they answer on the second guess they get only 5 points, third guess only 1 point. The winner is the group with the most points.

Game no. 88
What's In The Box?

Objective:	To practice Hebrew vocabulary
Suitable for Grades:	K - 3rd
Playing Time:	10 Minutes
Materials:	Different objects small enough to fit in a box
Grouping/Organization:	Large group
Variation:	Ask a volunteer to pick an item from the box and try to describe it for his friends, all in Hebrew.

Helpful Hints:

A great game for learning Hebrew and holiday vocabulary.

How to Play:

The teacher hides an object in a box. The teacher gives hints in Hebrew for the students to figure out the item. Hints can be things like shape, color, what we use it for, what sound it makes, etc. The students guess what's in the box.

If you keep a box of small treasures in the classroom you could play it so that when a student guesses the item, they get to keep the item. Alternatively, you can hand out a piece of candy for a right answer, or simply award points and the one with the most points wins a small prize.

Game no. 89
Hands Behind Your Back

Objective:	To practice conversational sentences in Hebrew
Suitable for Grades:	K - 3rd
Playing Time:	5 – 10 Minutes
Materials:	Different small objects
Grouping/Organization:	Large group

Helpful Hints:
This is a very funny game. Students just love it!

How to Play:
Students sit in a circle. The teacher picks a volunteer and gives them an object. The volunteer puts their hands behind their back and tries to describe what to do with the item without moving or showing with their hands.

It is surprising how many of us, students and adults alike, cannot talk without using our hands.

Game no. 90
Object Scavenger Hunt

Objective:	To practice Hebrew vocabulary
Suitable for Grades:	K – 6th
Playing Time:	10 Minutes
Materials:	Paper and pencils
Grouping/Organization:	3 Groups

Helpful Hints:

This is a great game for the beginning of the year, especially if students are getting to know a new school.

How to Play:

Divide the class into 3 groups. Each group is asked to make a list (in Hebrew) of things you can find in... Each group is assigned a different location: playground, hallway, the school gym, etc. When the students have made the list, they get 7 minutes to run quickly to this location and find the items on their list. If they are able to find those items at the location, the students check them off the list. The group that is back first, and has found all the items on the list, is the winner.

Game no. 91
That Reminds Me Of...

Objective:	To practice Hebrew conversation
Suitable for Grades:	K – 6th
Playing Time:	10 Minutes
Materials:	None
Grouping/Organization:	Large group

Helpful Hints:
Try to find a CD with different background sounds for this game.

How to Play:
Students sit in a circle. The teacher starts a sentence and says: "When I hear a ding-dong it reminds me of..." and then a student completes the sentence. If you can manage to find a CD with sound effects like a dog barking, a door creaking open, running water, and so on, it will really enhance this game.

You can also introduce other themes like:

"When I see the color red it makes me think of..."
"When I see a triangle it reminds me of...."

A good challenge is to ask one student to begin a sentence like that and another student to finish it.

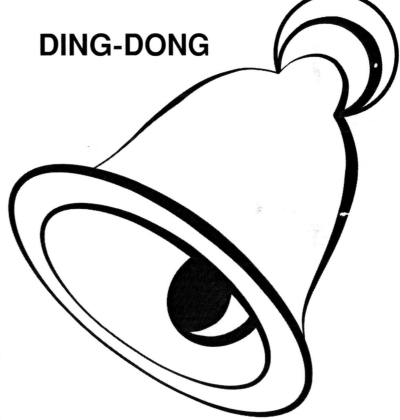

DING-DONG

Game no. 92
What's Missing?

Objective:	To practice basic Hebrew vocabulary
Suitable for Grades:	K – 3rd
Playing Time:	10 Minutes
Materials:	Flash cards with Hebrew words
Grouping/Organization:	Large group

Helpful Hints:

This is also a good game to play for memory practice.

How to Play:

Students sit in a circle. The teacher spreads flash cards on the floor in the middle of the circle, face up. There should be at least 20 cards but no more than 25 cards. Students have just 1 minute to memorize the cards. Then all the students close their eyes and the teacher pulls away one card. Students have to guess what card is missing.

Game no. 93
One Big Poster

Objective:	To practice Hebrew vocabulary and basic conversation
Suitable for Grades:	K - 3rd
Playing Time:	5 – 10 Minutes
Materials:	A big poster with a lot of pictures or details on it
Grouping/Organization:	Large group

Helpful Hints:
Just let the student's imagination run wild.

How to Play:
The teacher hangs a big poster on the board. Try to choose a "busy" poster with a lot of details. Students have 2 minutes to look at the poster before the teacher covers it. Then students describe what they saw in the poster. Usually the students' imagination helps them make up things. It is amusing to hear what they think they saw in the poster. When students have listed most of the things they can think of, uncover the poster and let them see the differences between what is really there and what they said. Good ideas for the poster are a farm scene, a busy intersection, and so on.

Game no. 94
What Was That Sound?

Objective: To practice basic Hebrew vocabulary
Suitable for Grades: K - 3rd
Playing Time: 5 – 10 Minutes
Materials: A wooden stick and some objects
Grouping/Organization: Large group

Helpful Hints:

A great, funny game.

How to Play:

Students sit in a circle and close their eyes. The teacher knocks with a wooden stick on an object in class. Students need to guess what the object is and say it in Hebrew. The object can be a book, a binder, a plastic cup, a glass dish, a metal spoon, etc. Look for objects that make different noises when you tap them.

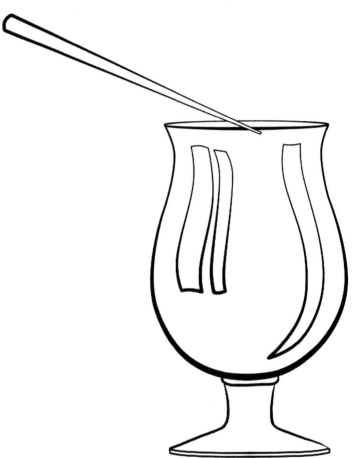

Game no. 95
A Ball Passes Through

Objective:	To practice Hebrew vocabulary and sentences
Suitable for Grades:	K - 3rd
Playing Time:	5 – 10 Minutes
Materials:	2 Balls, one for each group
Grouping/Organization:	2 Groups
Variations:	Instead of making a sentence, let each member say a word that begins with a specific letter (for example, everybody needs to say a word that begins with the letter "Tet" (ט'), or only words that belong to a specific family of words, etc.

Helpful Hints:

A great game for moving around and basic Hebrew sentences.

How to Play:

The teacher divides the class into 2 groups. Choose boys versus girls, groups divided by last names, or divide the class in the way you prefer. Each group stands in a line and students spread their legs and bend down with their arms between their legs. Each group gets a ball and the first word. Students pass the ball between their legs with their hands down the line to the next student. At the same time they add one word in Hebrew to complete a sentence. So the first student with the ball says a word, then the next student to get the ball adds a word to make a sentence. The next student adds one more word etc, so that they build a sentence that makes sense.

If a student is confused or repeats a word that has already been used, the ball is returned to the beginning of the line and you start the game over.

Game no. 96
Spelling Bear On The Tables

Objective:	To practice spelling words and decoding
Suitable for Grades:	K – 6th
Playing Time:	10 Minutes
Materials:	None
Grouping/Organization:	Individuals

Helpful Hints:
This game is fun and easy to play.

How to Play:
Students sit on the tables. The teacher says a word and asks a student to spell the word correctly. If the student gets the spelling wrong they go back to their chair. You can give students one or two chances if you like.

If a student who has been sent back to their chair knows the right spelling of another word, they can stand up and say: "spelling bears". The teacher then gives that student the opportunity to spell the word. If they are correct they get to go back and sit on the table.

101 - Let's have fun   Roni Rosenthal-Gazit

Game no. 97
The Opposite Game

Objective:	To practice basic Hebrew vocabulary
Suitable for Grades:	K – 1st
Playing Time:	10 Minutes
Materials:	Flash cards with Hebrew words
Grouping/Organization:	Individuals

Helpful Hints:

A fun and easy game.

How to Play:

The teacher gives each student a card with a word on it. Each student individually and silently attempts to find a card with a word opposite to the one on their card. When everyone is done, each student acts out their word pair and the others have to guess the words.

Game no. 98
The Ship

Objective:	To practice basic Hebrew vocabulary
Suitable for Grades:	K – 6th
Playing Time:	10 Minutes
Materials:	None
Grouping/Organization:	Large group

Helpful Hints:

A funny game.

How to Play:

Students stand in a circle. The teacher tells the students to imagine that they are standing on a boat. The teacher calls orders (in Hebrew), and signals a movement in response to the order, and everybody must follow along. The teacher keeps adding words and movements and tries to get the students confused. For example: when the teacher says "rock ahead", everybody has to cover their eyes. When the teacher says "shark attack", everybody starts swimming. When the teacher says "SOS", everybody has to signal with their hands, and when the teacher says "everybody take cover", all the students crouch down on the floor. Then the teacher tries to get the students confused by calling something but doing the wrong move. The students must listen to the order and do the correct move.

A student caught doing the wrong move is out. Last one playing is the winner.

Game no. 99
Write the Story

Objective:	To practice Hebrew writing
Suitable for Grades:	3rd – 6th
Playing Time:	10 Minutes
Materials:	A story in Hebrew
Grouping/Organization:	3 Groups

Helpful Hints:
This is a very creative game. The results can amaze you.

How to Play:
The teacher divides the class into 3 groups. Each group gets a story with one part of the story missing. Students fill out the missing part of the story. For example the first group gets a story without a beginning, the second group gets a story without a middle, and the third group gets a story without an ending. Each group completes the missing part. When all the re-written parts are put together, you get a whole new story. The outcome is really amazing.

???!!!???!!!

Game no. 100
A Whole New Story

Objective:	To practice Hebrew vocabulary
Suitable for Grades:	K – 8th
Playing Time:	10 Minutes
Materials:	Paper and pencils
Grouping/Organization:	3 - 4 Groups

Helpful Hints:
A creative and funny game.

How to Play:
The teacher divides the class into 3-4 groups, with no more than 4-5 students in a group. Each group gets a piece of paper and pencils to write with. The first student writes one sentence of a story and folds it, so the other students in their group cannot see what they wrote. The second student also writes one sentence, folds it, and so on for all the students in the group. When everybody has written something (you can have more than one turn), the student who wrote the first sentence unfolds the paper and reads the "new story" out loud.

Game no. 101
Describe It For Me, Please

Objective: To practice conversational Hebrew
Suitable for Grades: K – 6th
Playing Time: 10 Minutes
Materials: Paper and pencils
Grouping/Organization: Large group

Helpful Hints:
A funny game.

How to Play:
One student "a volunteer" stands in front of the class. They have to think about a character or an animal. The volunteer starts describing that character or animal to the class. The student cannot say what character or name it is. The students draw a picture of this character according to the volunteer's description. When the students are done, they present their art work to the class. Only then can the volunteer reveal the secret and reveal the name of the character or animal they were describing. Examples of characters are: a president, a famous singer, a popular model, etc.

Tips for teachers

- Games should be played in a fun and comfortable environment.
- If there are any "safety issues" at risk, do not play this particular game.
- Prizes can be symbolic and do not have to contain food. Be aware of food allergies.
- Each one of the games can be used as a model. Feel free to change the vocabulary suggested, use holiday vocabulary, or use the game for a different purpose. Be creative and remember to enjoy it yourself.
- Feel free to adjust the game to your students' Hebrew level.
- Don't let the game take over the lesson.
- Explain the rules of the game to the kids before you start playing.
- Always be positive. Even if a student does not win, don't let them get frustrated. Encourage them by telling them something like: "You did great, I'm not so sure that I could have done it better..."
- Don't let game go on too long. When you sense the children losing interest, it is time to stop.
- Expand on the idea that playing a game is not "free time"; they all need to be part of the game.
- Always keep games moving. If the kids lose interest, it's time to switch to a different game.
- For games where students are required to work in pairs or small groups, try to switch partners from time to time so that students don't get bored working with the same partner all the time.
- You can assign the groups or pairs beforehand so that students will know who they are expected to work with when they come to class.
- Make sure the students understand the assignments before you start the game. You could start out by saying something like: "Pretend I'm a new student, and tell me how to play this game.
- Encourage students to guess the correct answer even if they are not sure. Sometimes their "gut feeling" is correct, and they just lack confidence.
- The teacher should monitor the games at all times. Walk silently between the groups while they are working and listen to their conversations. Don't hesitate to jump in when a student is not tuned in.
- Encourage the kids to be creative. Children's imaginations are always developing. It's perfectly acceptable if the outcome of a game is different than what you had planned.
- You can be part of the game too. Enjoy.

נספח א'
אוסף דפי עבודה

אוֹצַר מִלִים

Draw a small picture for each one of the following items:

	אִשָּׁה	חָתוּל	סוּס	עַכְבָּר
	פָּרָה	כֶּלֶב	יֶלֶד	צִפּוֹר
	חָכָם	רַעַשׁ	מִשְׁפָּחָה	בַּיִת
	אִישׁ	סַבָּא	שָׁלוֹם	שֶׁקֶט
	אֹהֶל	אֹכֶל	יַלְדָּה	עוֹרֵב

אוֹצַר מִלִּים וּכְתִיבַת מִשְׁפָּטִים

1. Draw a small picture for each one of the following items and answer the following questions:

מֶלֶךְ	דְּבוֹרָה	שֻׁלְחָן	עִיר
פֶּרַח	יְרָקוֹת	בֵּיצָה	מִטְרִיָּה
דְּבַשׁ	כֶּלֶב	בֵּית הַמִּקְדָּשׁ	פַּרְפַּר

2. Write 3 sentences using the pictures above

1._____

2._____

3._____

3. What is the connection between 3 out of the 9 pictures (above this question) and Jerusalem?

_____

_____

_____

_____

4. What is the connection between 4 out of the 9 pictures (above) and Passover?

_____

_____

_____

_____

מִלּוֹת יַחַס

Draw a small picture to exemplify the meaning of the preposition words in the table:

בֵּין		עַל-יָד	
תַּחַת		עַל	
אַחֲרֵי		לִפְנֵי	
אֶל		בְּתוֹךְ	
אֵצֶל		עִם	

Write sentences for each one of the preposition words:

1 עַל-יָד - _____

2 בֵּין - _____

3 עַל - _____

4 תַּחַת - _____

5 לִפְנֵי - _____

6 אַחֲרֵי - _____

7 בְּתוֹךְ - _____

8 אֶל - _____

9 עִם - _____

10 אֵצֶל - _____

מִמִּלִים לְמִשְׁפָּטִים

Put these words into sentences

מִלִים

שֶׁקֶט	עָלִים	קוֹרֵא	בּוֹכֶה	גְּבִינָה	תַּפּוּחַ	יָרֵחַ	לוֹקֵחַ
רוֹאָה	גָּרָה	שׁוֹמֵעַ	רוֹצֶה	אוֹכֵל	כָּאן	אוֹהֲבִים	פֶּרַח
עֵצִים	עוֹמֵד	הַרְבֵּה	נִדְנֵדָה	כִּסֵּא	שֻׁלְחָן	עֵט	עוּגִיּוֹת
			רוֹצִים	סֵפֶר	בַּבַּיִת	לֶחֶם	כּוֹס

מִשְׁפָּטִים

_____   יֵשׁ לִי   1

_____   אֵין לְךָ   2

_____   אֲנִי   3

_____   הוּא   4

_____   הִיא   5

_____   הֵם   6

_____ ?   לָמָה אַתָּה   7

_____ עַל הַ _____   הַ   8

_____ תַּחַת _____   הַ   9

_____ לִפְנֵי _____   הַ   10

_____ אַחֲרֵי _____   הַ   11

_____ בְּתוֹךְ הַ _____   הַ   12

מִשְׁפָּטִים מְבֻלְבָּלִים

We are so mixed up; try to organize us so that we form a sentence (follow the example):

Sentences = מִשְׁפָּטִים	Words = מִלִים
אֲנִי רוֹצָה לִשְׁתּוֹת מַיִם בְּבַקָשָׁה EXAMPLE	מַיִם, אֲנִי, רוֹצָה, בְּבַקָשָׁה, לִשְׁתּוֹת
	רַבָּה, תּוֹדָה, לְךָ
	מְאֹד, קַר, בַּחֹרֶף
	יֵשׁ, עַל, הַכִּסֵּא, צַלַחַת
	בַּחֹרֶף, גֶּשֶׁם, יוֹרֵד
	בַּקַּיִץ, הוֹלְכִים, לַיָּם
	ט"ו בִּשְׁבָט, חַג, לָאִילָנוֹת

Some sentences can be written in more than one correct way. Put those words into sentences in 2 different ways:

כֶּלֶב, הָעֵץ, עוֹמֵד, עַל-יָד

1. _____

2. _____

Now you try: write 3 scrambled sentences in Hebrew and organize them in the right order

Sentences = מִשְׁפָּטִים	Words = מִלִים

לְכָל אוֹת מִלָּה

1. Write a word that begins with each one of the following letters:

א _____

ב _____

ה _____

ז _____

ל _____

מ _____

נ _____

ע _____

צ _____

ק _____

ש _____

ת _____

2. Write a word that ends with the following letters:

1. _____ן

2. _____ם

3. _____ו

4. _____ף

5. _____ץ

3. Now, try to form those words into sentences:

1. _____

2. _____

מְצָא אֶת הָאוֹת שֶׁנָּפְלָה – אוֹצַר מִלִּים

The following words are missing a letter. Try to fill in the blanks and find the missing letter. Copy the word you found. (A helpful hint: you might find more than one correct answer).

_____	שֻׁלְ_ָן	1
_____	כִּ_א	2
_____	_רוֹן	3
_____	בָּ_וֹן	4
_____	פַּרְפָּ_	5
_____	_לֵב	6
_____	סֵ_ר	7
_____	מַחְבַּר_	8
_____	חֲבָ_ה	9
_____	דְּל_	10
_____	חַלּוֹ_	11
_____	_לְקוֹט	12
_____	_לָדִים	13
_____	מִשְׂחָק_ם	14
_____	עֲנָבִ_	15

סִפּוּר חָסֵר

Read the story and fill in the blank space (the word is given to you in English):

(school)_____ _____ כְּשֶׁהָיָה הוֹלֵךְ לְ יוֹתָם אָהַב מְאֹד טִיּוּלִים. בְּכָל בֹּקֶר,

(surprise)_____ הָיָה מְקַוֶּה שֶׁהַמּוֹרָה תּוֹדִיעַ עַל הַטִּיּוּל הַבָּא. הַבֹּקֶר חִכְּתָה לְיוֹתָם

(trip)_____ הַקָּרוֹב, וּבִקְשָׁה שֶׁהוֹרֶה יְלַוֶּה אֶת הַטִּיּוּל. הַמּוֹרָה חֶדְוָה הוֹדִיעָה עַל הַ

(dad)_____ אוֹ (mom)_____ יוֹתָם קִוָּה שֶׁ יַסְכִּימוּ לָצֵאת אִתּוֹ לַטִּיּוּל.

(run)_____ (home)_____ הַ מִיָּד, לְחַפֵּשׂ אֶת וְלָכֵן, כְּשֶׁחָזַר יוֹתָם אֶל

(parents)_____ הַ שֶׁלּוֹ.

(disappointed)_____), כִּי אִמָּא שֶׁל יוֹתָם הָיְתָה _____ יוֹתָם הָיָה מְאֹד

(sick)_____ וְשָׁכְבָה בַּ _____ (bed).

(work)_____ (said): "אֲנִי מִצְטַעֵר. יֵשׁ לִי הַרְבֵּה _____ אַבָּא שֶׁל יוֹתָם

וְלֹא אוּכַל לָבוֹא אִתְּךָ לַטִּיּוּל".

(sad)_____), וְלֹא יָדַע מָה לַעֲשׂוֹת. "יוֹתָם הָיָה

(sister)_____ הַגְּדוֹלָה שֶׁל יוֹתָם, אָמְרָה: «אַל תִּדְאַג יוֹתָם, אֲנִי אָבוֹא אִתְּךָ יָעֵל,

(love)_____ טִיּוּלִים. הֲכִי אֲנִי אוֹהֶבֶת לְטַפֵּס עַל ה לַטִּיּוּל. אֲנִי

(mountain)_____ וְלִרְאוֹת אֶת הַנּוֹף".

יוֹתָם שָׂמַח מְאֹד.

אִפְיוּן מִלִים עַל פִּי תְכוּנוֹת

Place those items into the matching place in the table below (classify). Follow the example:

שֻׁלְחָן, כִּסֵא, בַּקְבּוּק, שְׂחִיָּה, שֶׁמֶשׁ, מְנוֹרָה, סֵפֶר, אֹרֶז, יַלְדָּה, שָׁעוֹן, פֶּרַח, פַּרְפַּר, צִפּוֹר, סוּס, מִסְעָדָה, בֻּבָּה, גֶּזֶר, עַגְבָנִיָּה, מְשֻׁלָּשׁ, לָבָן, כָּחֹל, דָּג, דְּבַשׁ, הַר, חָלָב, יָד, רֹאשׁ, רֶגֶל, כַּדּוּר, כֶּלֶב, לֵב, נֵר, עֵץ, לְצַיֵּר, לְדַבֵּר, לִרְקֹד.

אַחֵר	דְּבָרִים שֶׁכֵּיף לַעֲשׂוֹת	דְּבָרִים שֶׁאֶפְשָׁר לֶאֱכֹל	דְּבָרִים עֲגֻלִּים	דְּבָרִים בְּצֶבַע צָהֹב

שִׂיחָה, הֲבָנָה וּכְתִיבָה
שְׁאֵלוֹן לְחָבֵר/ לַחֲבֵרָה

Interview a friend and write down the answers in Hebrew.

1. מַה הַשֵׁם שֶׁלְךָ/שֶׁלָךְ?

_____

2. אֵיזֶה צֶבַע אַתְּ/אַתָּה אוֹהֵב/אוֹהֶבֶת?

_____

3. מָה אַתְּ/אַתָּה אוֹהֵב/אוֹהֶבֶת לַעֲשׂוֹת?

_____

4. מָתַי יוֹם הַהֻלֶדֶת שֶׁלְךָ/שֶׁלָךְ?

_____

5. אֵיפֹה נוֹלַדְתָּ/נוֹלַדְתְּ?

_____

6. אֵיזֶה יוֹם בַּשָׁבוּעַ אַתְּ/אַתָּה הֲכִי אוֹהֵב/אוֹהֶבֶת?

_____

7. אֵיזֶה בַּעַל חַיִים אַתְּ/אַתָּה אוֹהֵב/אוֹהֶבֶת?

_____

8. אֵיזֶה מוּסִיקָה אַתְּ/אַתָּה אוֹהֵב/אוֹהֶבֶת לִשְׁמֹעַ?

_____

9. מָה אַתְּ/אַתָּה אוֹהֵב/אוֹהֶבֶת לִלְמֹד?

_____

10. מַה הַתַּחְבִּיב שֶׁלְךָ/שֶׁלָךְ?

_____

11. מָה אַתְּ/אַתָּה אוֹהֵב/אוֹהֶבֶת לַעֲשׂוֹת בַּקַיִץ?

_____

12. מָה אַתְּ/אַתָּה אוֹהֵב/אוֹהֶבֶת לֶאֱכֹל?

_____

13. מָה אַתְּ/אַתָּה אוֹהֵב/אוֹהֶבֶת לִשְׁתוֹת?

_____

14. מָה הָיִיתָ/הָיִית רוֹצֶה/רוֹצָה לְקַבֵּל בְּמַתָּנָה?

_____

15. אֵילוּ סְפָרִים אַתְּ/אַתָּה אוֹהֵב/אוֹהֶבֶת לִקְרֹא?

_____

Now, add 8 questions on your own.

הִשְׁתַּמֵּשׁ בְּמִלּוֹת הַשְּׁאֵלָה:

מִי, מַה, לָמָה, כֵּיצַד, מָתַי, אֵיךְ, אֵיפֹה, כַּמָּה, אֵיזֶה, לְאָן

_____ ?	_____	16
_____ ?	_____	17
_____ ?	_____	18
_____ ?	_____	19
_____ ?	_____	20
_____ ?	_____	21
_____ ?	_____	22
_____ ?	_____	23

מָה אֲנִי לוֹמֵד/ לוֹמֶדֶת בְּבֵית הַסֵּפֶר?

Draw a line between the subject you learn in school and its matching description.

לָרוּץ וְלִקְפֹּץ	הִסְטוֹרְיָה
מַה שֶׁעָשִׂינוּ בֶּעָבָר	אַנְגְּלִית
לִסְפֹּר וּלְחַבֵּר מִסְפָּרִים	עִבְרִית
לִקְרֹא א-ב	טֶבַע
אוֹתִיּוֹת ABC	חֶשְׁבּוֹן
חַיּוֹת, פְּרָחִים וְעֵצִים	הִתְעַמְּלוּת
עַל בְּנֵי יִשְׂרָאֵל וְעַל אֱלֹקִים	מַחְשְׁבִים
לְהַקְלִיד אוֹתִיּוֹת	חַגִּים
מַה חוֹגְגִים, לָמָה וּמָתַי	תּוֹרָה

תִּפְזֹרֶת מִלִּים

Here is a word search puzzle. Find these words in the puzzle.

מְכוֹנִית, מִרְפָּאָה, מְכוֹנִית כִּבּוּי אֵשׁ, מָסוֹק, אוֹפַנּוֹעַ, אָחוֹת, טַיָּס, מוֹרֶה, דּוֹאַר, בֵּית סֵפֶר, נַגָּר, צַיֶּרֶת, מְנַהֵל, רוֹפֵא עוֹר, מוֹכֵר.

ע	ה	א	פ	ר	מ
ץ	פ	ח	ט	ו	כ
כ	ד	ו	א	פ	ו
מ	ו	ת	כ	א	נ
ע	ו	פ	ץ	ע	י
מ	ר	ד	ג	ו	ת
ו	ב	מ	א	ר	כ
ר	פ	ס	ת	י	ב
ה	שׁ	ו	שׁ	ט	ו
י	ק	ק	ב	ד	י
ע	ו	נ	פ	ו	א
ו	ן	ה	צ	א	שׁ
פ	ם	ת	ט	ר	ל
ת	ת	ר	י	צ	י
מ	ת	צ	ס	ץ	ף
ל	ד	ג	ס	י	ח
ה	ט	ר	כ	ו	מ
נ	ע	י	כ	ו	ד
מ	כ	ו	נ	י	ת
ר	א	ט	ר	ג	נ

שְׁאַל אֶת עַצְמְךָ

Ask yourself the following questions and write your answers in the sentences.

1. מָה אֲנִי אוֹהֵב/ אוֹהֶבֶת לַעֲשׂוֹת?
_____

מִפְּנֵי שֶׁ _____ אֲנִי אוֹהֵב/ אוֹהֶבֶת לְ
_____

2. מָה אֲנִי לֹא אוֹהֵב/ אוֹהֶבֶת לַעֲשׂוֹת?
_____

כִּי _____ אֲנִי לֹא אוֹהֵב/ אוֹהֶבֶת
_____

3. מֶה הָיִיתִי רוֹצֶה/ רוֹצָה לִהְיוֹת?
_____

כְּדֵי שֶׁ _____ הָיִיתִי רוֹצֶה/רוֹצָה לִהְיוֹת
_____

4. מַשֶּׁהוּ שֶׁאַף פַּעַם לֹא הָיִיתִי עוֹשֶׂה/ עוֹשָׂה:
_____

כִּי _____ לֹא הָיִיתִי _____
_____

5. מַה הַסּוֹד שֶׁלִּי?
_____

אַל תְּגַלּוּ לְאַף אֶחָד, אֲבָל הַסּוֹד שֶׁלִּי הוּא
_____

כָּכָה אֲנִי נִרְאֶה/ נִרְאֵית כְּשֶׁאֲנִי......

Draw yourself doing these activities.

	1	כָּכָה אֲנִי נִרְאֶה כְּשֶׁאֲנִי רוֹכֵב עַל אוֹפַנַּיִם אוֹ: כָּכָה אֲנִי נִרְאֵית כְּשֶׁאֲנִי רוֹכֶבֶת עַל אוֹפַנַּיִם.
	2	כָּכָה אֲנִי נִרְאֶה כְּשֶׁאֲנִי אוֹכֵל אֲרוּחַת צָהֳרַיִם. אוֹ: כָּכָה אֲנִי נִרְאֵית כְּשֶׁאֲנִי אוֹכֶלֶת אֲרוּחַת צָהֳרַיִם.
	3	כָּכָה אֲנִי נִרְאֶה כְּשֶׁאֲנִי יָשֵׁן. אוֹ: כָּכָה אֲנִי נִרְאֵית כְּשֶׁאֲנִי יְשֵׁנָה.
	4	כָּכָה אֲנִי נִרְאֶה כְּשֶׁאֲנִי רוֹקֵד. אוֹ: כָּכָה אֲנִי נִרְאֵית כְּשֶׁאֲנִי רוֹקֶדֶת.

הַחֲבֵרִים שֶׁלִּי בַּכִּתָּה

Find a classmate for each one of the categories below.
Ask him/her to sign their name.

אוֹהֵב/ אוֹהֶבֶת לִשְׂחוֹת	הָיָה/ הָיְתָה בְּבֵית מָלוֹן
יֵשׁ לוֹ/לָהּ כֶּלֶב	רָאָה/ רָאֲתָה סֶרֶט בַּקּוֹלְנוֹעַ
יֵשׁ לוֹ/לָהּ כַּדּוּר	אֲנִי מַכִּיר אוֹתוֹ/ אוֹתָהּ הֲכִי הַרְבֵּה זְמַן
נָסַע/נָסְעָה לְאֶרֶץ אַחֶרֶת	יֵשׁ לוֹ/לָהּ עֵינַיִם יְרֻקּוֹת
אוֹהֵב/ אוֹהֶבֶת לָשִׁיר	יֵשׁ לוֹ/לָהּ חֻלְצָה בְּצֶבַע חוּם
יֵשׁ לוֹ/לָהּ כְּפָפוֹת לְבָנוֹת	יֵשׁ לוֹ/לָהּ שְׂעָרוֹת אֲרֻכּוֹת
אוֹהֵב/אוֹהֶבֶת לִקְרֹא	אוֹהֵב/אוֹהֶבֶת לְשַׂחֵק בְּכַדּוּר

מִי רוֹצֶה לִהְיוֹת....?

Interview your friends and write down their name(s) next to the profession.

_____	_____	1 מִי רוֹצֶה לִהְיוֹת טַיָּס?
_____	_____	2 מִי רוֹצֶה לִהְיוֹת טַיֶּסֶת?
_____	_____	3 מִי רוֹצֶה לִהְיוֹת מוֹרֶה?
_____	_____	4 מִי רוֹצֶה לִהְיוֹת מוֹרָה?
_____	_____	5 מִי רוֹצֶה לִהְיוֹת רוֹפֵא?
_____	_____	6 מִי רוֹצֶה לִהְיוֹת רוֹפְאָה?
_____	_____	7 מִי רוֹצֶה לִהְיוֹת שֶׁף בְּמִסְעָדָה?
_____	_____	8 מִי רוֹצֶה לִהְיוֹת שֶׁפִית בְּמִסְעָדָה?
_____	_____	9 מִי רוֹצֶה לִהְיוֹת שׁוֹטֵר?
_____	_____	10 מִי רוֹצֶה לִהְיוֹת שׁוֹטֶרֶת?
_____	_____	11 מִי רוֹצֶה לִהְיוֹת זַמָּר?
_____	_____	12 מִי רוֹצֶה לִהְיוֹת זַמֶּרֶת?
_____	_____	13 מִי רוֹצֶה לִהְיוֹת טַיַּס חָלָל?
_____	_____	14 מִי רוֹצֶה לִהְיוֹת טַיֶּסֶת חָלָל?
_____	_____	15 מִי רוֹצֶה לִהְיוֹת כַּבַּאי?
_____	_____	16 מִי רוֹצֶה לִהְיוֹת כַּבָּאִית?
_____	_____	17 מִי רוֹצֶה לִהְיוֹת צַיָּר?
_____	_____	18 מִי רוֹצֶה לִהְיוֹת צַיֶּרֶת?

חִידוֹן בִּתְמוּנוֹת

Answer the following riddles and draw the pictures inside the square.

	1. הִיא עֲגֻלָּה וּצְהֻבָּה. בַּשָּׁמַיִם הִיא נוֹתֶנֶת אוֹר. רֶמֶז: מַתְחִיל בְּאוֹת שׁ׳...
	2. יֵשׁ לוֹ אַרְבַּע רַגְלַיִם. יוֹשְׁבִים עָלָיו וְהוּא נוֹחַ. רֶמֶז: מַתְחִיל בְּאוֹת כּ׳...
	3. תּוֹלִים אוֹתָהּ עַל הַקִּיר. הִיא יָפָה, וְנָעִים לְהִסְתַּכֵּל עָלֶיהָ. רֶמֶז: מַתְחִיל בְּאוֹת ת׳...
	4. הוּא מַשְׁמִיעַ קוֹל: תִּיק-תַּק, תִּיק-תַּק. הוּא לֹא עוֹצֵר אַף פַּעַם. רֶמֶז: מַתְחִיל בְּאוֹת שׁ׳...

חִידוֹן חַיּוֹת

Which animal is hiding in the riddle?

	1. אֲנִי לְבָנָה וְעָפָה בַּשָּׁמַיִם. יֵשׁ לִי מַקּוֹר אָרֹךְ וַאֲנִי בּוֹנָה קֵן. אֲנִי מְבִיאָה אֶת הַשָּׁלוֹם. רֶמֶז: מַתְחִיל בָּאוֹת י׳...
	2. אֲנִי גָּרָה בָּרֶפֶת. אֲנִי נוֹתֶנֶת חָלָב. אֲנִי אוֹמֶרֶת: מוּ, מוּ. רֶמֶז: מַתְחִיל בָּאוֹת פ׳...
	4. אֲנִי גָּר בָּאֲרֻוָה. אֲנִי גָּדוֹל וְחָזָק. אֲנִי אוֹהֵב לִדְהֹר. רֶמֶז: מַתְחִיל בָּאוֹת ס׳...
	5. אֲנִי גָּרָה בַּלוּל. אֲנִי נוֹתֶנֶת בֵּיצִים. יֵשׁ לִי כַּרְבֹּלֶת וַאֲנִי אוֹמֶרֶת: קוּ-קוּ-רִי-קוּ רֶמֶז: מַתְחִיל בָּאוֹת ת׳...

סֶקֶר בַּכִּתָּה

Interview your friends and write down their answers in the right place.

•מַה הַסְּפּוֹרְט שֶׁהֵם הֲכִי אוֹהֲבִים?
•מַה הַפְּרִי שֶׁהֵם הֲכִי אוֹהֲבִים?
•מַהִי הָעוֹנָה (קַיִץ, סְתָו, חֹרֶף, אָבִיב) שֶׁהֵם הֲכִי אוֹהֲבִים?

הָעוֹנָה (קַיִץ, סְתָו, חֹרֶף, אָבִיב) שֶׁהֵם הֲכִי אוֹהֲבִים	הַפְּרִי שֶׁהֵם הֲכִי אוֹהֲבִים	הַסְּפּוֹרְט שֶׁהֵם הֲכִי אוֹהֲבִים	שֵׁם הֶחָבֵר

גִּימַטְרִיָּא

In Gematria each letter gets a numerical value. Find out the following words:

10 + 50 + 1

— — —

50+6+30+8

— — — —

5+4+30+10

— — — —

Now, it's your turn to try. Find the mathematical valuation of each letter in the following sentences:

אֲנִי רוֹצֶה לֶאֱכֹל גְּלִידָה

— — — — — — — — — —

— — — — —

תִּפְתַּח אֶת הַחַלוֹן, בְּבַקָּשָׁה

— — — — — — — — — —

·— — — — —

אַל תִּשְׁכַּח לְהָבִיא חָלָב

— — — — — — — — —

·— — —

חַג פּוּרִים הוּא חַג נֶחְמָד

— — — — — — — — — — —

·— — — —

אֲנִי רוֹצֶה לִשְׁתּוֹת מַיִם, בְּבַקָּשָׁה

— — — — — — — — — —

— — — — —,— — —

חֶשְׁבּוֹן בְּעִבְרִית

Write this math exercise into words:

	הֵם		וְעוֹד	$2 + 3 = 5$
	הֵם		כָּפוּל	$4 \times 4 = 16$
	הֵם		חֶלְקֵי	$9:9 = 1$
	הֵם		פָּחוֹת	$8-2 = 6$
	הֵם		וְעוֹד	$16 + 12 = 28$
	הֵם		כָּפוּל	$8 \times 4 = 32$
	הֵם		חֶלְקֵי	$15:3 = 5$
	הֵם		פָּחוֹת	$48 - 8 = 40$
		קָטָן מֵ		$10 > 5$
		גָּדוֹל מֵ		$7 < 12$
שָׁוֶה לְ		וְעוֹד		$20 + 6 = 23 + 3$
		וְעוֹד		
שָׁוֶה לְ		פָּחוֹת		$43 - 7 = 45-9$
		פָּחוֹת		

לְכָל שְׁאֵלָה תְּשׁוּבָה.

Write the matching question to each answer.

_____

תְּשׁוּבָה: כֵּן, אֲנִי גָּר בְּחֵיפָה.

_____

תְּשׁוּבָה: לֹא, אֲנִי לֹא אוֹהֶבֶת לִשְׂחוֹת בַּיָּם.

_____

תְּשׁוּבָה: לֹא. נִגְמְרוּ הָעַגְבָנִיּוֹת בַּמְּקָרֵר.

_____

תְּשׁוּבָה: בִּירוּשָׁלַיִם.

_____

תְּשׁוּבָה: אֲנִי לֹא יוֹדַעַת. הוּא לֹא אָמַר.

_____

תְּשׁוּבָה: כֵּן, אֲנִי חוֹשֵׁב שֶׁזֶּה יִהְיֶה נֶהְדָּר.

_____

תְּשׁוּבָה: כֵּן, בְּשִׂמְחָה.

_____

תְּשׁוּבָה: כִּי יֵשׁ לִי יוֹם הוּלֶדֶת הַיּוֹם.

_____

תְּשׁוּבָה: לֹא מָחָר. כִּי מָחָר יוֹם חֲמִישִׁי.

כְּתִיבָה וַהֲבָנָה

Fill in the missing sentences in the dialog:

_____

אֱיָל: "שָׁלוֹם אַיָלָה, מַה שְׁלוֹמֵךְ?"

_____

אֱיָל: "אֲנִי כָּל כָּךְ שָׂמֵחַ. חָשַׁשְׁתִּי שֶׁנֵּאָלֵץ לְבַטֵּל אֶת הַטִּיּוּל".

_____

אֱיָל: "כֵּן, נֵצֵא בְּיוֹם רְבִיעִי בְּשָׁעָה שְׁמוֹנֶה בַּבֹּקֶר".

_____

אֱיָל: "כֵּן, הַכֹּל כְּבָר מוּכָן. אֲרַזְתִּי קֻפְסָאוֹת שֶׁל אֹכֶל וְהַרְבֵּה שְׁתִיָּה לְכֻלָּם".

_____

אֱיָל: "אֲנִי חוֹשֵׁב שֶׁלֹּא. בְּגָדִים קְצָרִים זֶה יִהְיֶה בְּסֵדֶר גָּמוּר".

_____

אֱיָל: "כֵּן, אֲנִי מַסְכִּים. אֲנִי חוֹשֵׁב שֶׁזֶּה רַעְיוֹן טוֹב".

_____

אֱיָל: "נַחֲזֹר עַד שֶׁבַע בָּעֶרֶב".

_____

אֱיָל: "לֹא, אֵין צֹרֶךְ, אֲנִי אָבִיא מַסְפִּיק מַטְבְּעוֹת בִּשְׁבִיל כֻּלָּם".

_____

אֱיָל: "מְצֻיָּן. אָז קָבַעְנוּ. יוֹם רְבִיעִי בְּשָׁעָה שְׁמוֹנֶה בַּבֹּקֶר, לְיַד הַחֲנוּת שֶׁל מֹשֶׁה".

_____

אֱיָל: "לְהִתְרָאוֹת".

תַּרְגִּיל בִּכְתִיבָה

Write an ending to the stories:

"רִינָה מְאֹד הִתְרַגְּשָׁה. הַכַּלְבָּה שֶׁלָּהֶם, מִימִי, עָמְדָה לְהַמְלִיט גּוּרִים בְּכָל רֶגַע. עוֹד בַּבֹּקֶר, לִפְנֵי שֶׁהָלְכָה לְבֵית הַסֵּפֶר, אָמְרָה רִינָה לְאִמָּא, שֶׁהַיּוֹם יֵשׁ לָהּ הַרְגָּשָׁה שֶׁזֶּה יִקְרֶה. שֶׁעוֹד הַיּוֹם, סוֹף סוֹף, יֵצְאוּ מֵהַבֶּטֶן שֶׁל מִימִי גּוּרִים חֲמוּדִים וּלְבָנִים.

אֲבָל, כְּשֶׁחָזְרָה רִינָה מִבֵּית הַסֵּפֶר וּפָתְחָה אֶת הַדֶּלֶת, חִכְּתָה לָהּ הַפְתָּעָה"......

סוֹף הַסִּפּוּר: _____

_____

_____

_____

"יוֹתָם אָהַב מְאֹד לִקְפֹּץ עַל הַטְּרַמְפּוֹלִינָה שֶׁלּוֹ בֶּחָצֵר. בְּכָל יוֹם כְּשֶׁהָיָה חוֹזֵר מֵהַגַּן, הָיָה מְמַהֵר אֶל הֶחָצֵר. אִמָּא חָשְׁשָׁה מְאֹד. "אַתָּה חַיָּב לְהִזָּהֵר" הִיא בִּקְשָׁה. בְּדֶרֶךְ כְּלָל הָיָה יוֹתָם זָהִיר. אֶלָּא שֶׁהַיּוֹם, קָרָה מַשֶּׁהוּ מוּזָר..."

סוֹף הַסִּפּוּר:

_____

_____

_____

_____

מַטְּלוֹת כְּתִיבָה

Write advertisements according to the following stories.

1. רָן רוֹצֶה לִמְכֹּר אֶת הָאוֹפַנַּיִם שֶׁלּוֹ. הוּא קִבֵּל אוֹתָם בְּמַתָּנָה לְיוֹם הַהֻלֶּדֶת לִפְנֵי שְׁנָתַיִם, כְּשֶׁהָיוּ חֲדָשִׁים. הָאוֹפַנַּיִם בְּמַצָּב טוֹב, בְּצֶבַע אָדֹם, אֲבָל הֵם מַתְאִימִים לִילָדִים בְּגִיל שְׁמוֹנֶה, וְאִלּוּ רָן כְּבָר כִּמְעַט בֶּן עֶשֶׂר.

עִזְרוּ לְרָן לִכְתֹּב מוֹדָעָה לִמְכִירַת הָאוֹפַנַּיִם שֶׁלּוֹ.

_____

_____

_____

_____

_____

2. אִמָּא שֶׁל חַנִּי מְחַפֶּשֶׂת עוֹזֵר אוֹ עוֹזֶרֶת לְמֶשֶׁק בַּיִת, לְעֶזְרָה בַּעֲבוֹדוֹת נִקְיוֹן הַבַּיִת, בְּבִשּׁוּל, בִּכְבִיסָה וּבִרְחִיצַת הַכֵּלִים. חָשׁוּב לָהּ שֶׁהָעוֹזֵר אוֹ הָעוֹזֶרֶת יִהְיוּ אַחְרָאִיִּים, מְסֻדָּרִים וְלֹא מְעַשְּׁנִים, וְשֶׁיָּגוּרוּ בְּאֵזוֹר נְתַנְיָה.
אִמָּא שֶׁל חַנִּי תִּשְׂמַח לְעֶזְרָה בִּימֵי שִׁשִּׁי בַּבֹּקֶר.

עִזְרוּ לְאִמָּא שֶׁל חַנִּי לִכְתֹּב מוֹדַעַת "דְּרוּשִׁים".

_____

_____

_____

_____

_____

סִפּוּר חָסֵר

Fill in the missing sentence in the story.

סִפּוּר מִסְפָּר 1

דָּנִי מִתְעוֹרֵר בְּכָל יוֹם בְּשָׁעָה 7 בְּדִיּוּק. דָּבָר רִאשׁוֹן הוּא רוֹחֵץ פָּנִים וּמְצַחְצֵחַ שִׁנַּיִם. אַחַר כָּךְ הוּא _____

וּלְבַסּוֹף נוֹעֵל אֶת נְעָלָיו וְהוֹלֵךְ לְבֵית הַסֵּפֶר.

סִפּוּר מִסְפָּר 2

עִנְבָּל אוֹהֶבֶת לְשַׂחֵק עִם שַׁחַר. בְּכָל יוֹם אַחֲרֵי הַגַּן נִפְגָּשׁוֹת שְׁתֵּי הַחֲבֵרוֹת וּמְבַלּוֹת בְּמֶשֶׁךְ כָּל אַחַר-הַצָּהֳרַיִם יַחַד. אֶלָּא שֶׁהַיּוֹם הַבָּנוֹת לֹא יְכוֹלוֹת לְהִפָּגֵשׁ. הַיּוֹם עִנְבָּל צְרִיכָה לָלֶכֶת לְ _____

לֹא נוֹרָא, מָחָר שׁוּב יַחְזְרוּ לְשַׂחֵק יַחַד.

סִפּוּר מִסְפָּר 3

הַטֶּלֶפוֹן צִלְצֵל וְנוּרִית מִהֲרָה לַעֲנוֹת. אִמָּא הִתְקַשְּׁרָה מֵהַמִּשְׂרָד וְאָמְרָה שֶׁ _____

_____

נוּרִית כְּבָר לֹא יָכְלָה לְחַכּוֹת, וּכְשֶׁאִמָּא נִכְנְסָה הַבַּיְתָה הִיא מִהֲרָה וְחִבְּקָה אֶת אִמָּא בְּשִׂמְחָה.

סִפּוּר מִסְפָּר 4

שַׁחַר הִיא הָאָחוֹת הַגְּדוֹלָה שֶׁל לִיאוֹר. שַׁחַר וְלִיאוֹר מְאֹד אוֹהֲבִים אֶחָד אֶת הַשֵּׁנִי וְנֶהֱנִים לְשַׂחֵק יַחְדָּו. אֶלָּא שֶׁהַיּוֹם בַּצָּהֳרַיִם כְּשֶׁשַּׁחַר חָזְרָה מִבֵּית הַסֵּפֶר הִיא גִּלְּתָה שֶׁלִּיאוֹר _____

_____

לִיאוֹר בָּכָה וּבִקֵּשׁ סְלִיחָה וְשַׁחַר כַּמּוּבָן סָלְחָה לוֹ וְחִבְּקָה אוֹתוֹ.

דּו-שִׂיחַ דִּמְיוֹנִי

Fill in the missing sentences they would say if they could talk.

אִם כֶּלֶב וְחָתוּל הָיוּ יְכוֹלִים לְדַבֵּר, אָז הֵם הָיוּ אוֹמְרִים:

הַכֶּלֶב: _____

הֶחָתוּל: _____

אִם הַשֶּׁמֶשׁ וְהַיָּרֵחַ הָיוּ יְכוֹלִים לְדַבֵּר, אָז הֵם הָיוּ אוֹמְרִים:

הַשֶּׁמֶשׁ: _____

הַיָּרֵחַ: _____

אִם הַפֶּרַח וְהַפַּרְפַּר הָיוּ יְכוֹלִים לְדַבֵּר, אָז הֵם הָיוּ אוֹמְרִים:

הַפֶּרַח: _____

הַפַּרְפַּר: _____

אִם הַשְּׂרוֹכִים וְהַנַּעֲלַיִם הָיוּ יְכוֹלִים לְדַבֵּר, אָז הֵם הָיוּ אוֹמְרִים:

הַשְּׂרוֹכִים: _____

הַנַּעֲלַיִם: _____

אִם הַמַּפְתֵּחַ וְהַדֶּלֶת הָיוּ יְכוֹלִים לְדַבֵּר, אָז הֵם הָיוּ אוֹמְרִים:

הַמַּפְתֵּחַ: _____

הַדֶּלֶת: _____

אָז מָה הַמְּשִׂימָה?

Read the following assignments and try to carry them out:

1. צַיֵּר חֲמִשָּׁה עֲגוּלִים וּצְבַע אוֹתָם בְּוָרֹד.

2. קְפֹץ עַל רֶגֶל אַחַת שֶׁבַע פְּעָמִים.

3. שִׂים אֶת הָעִפָּרוֹן עַל הָאַף.

4. שְׁרֹק שִׁיר שֶׁאַתָּה אוֹהֵב.

5. אֱמֹר שָׁלוֹם לְחָבֵר שֶׁיּוֹשֵׁב לְיָדְךָ.

6. צַיֵּר מָטוֹס עַל דַּף.

7. הַקֵּף אֶת הַכִּסֵּא שֶׁלְּךָ שְׁמוֹנֶה פְּעָמִים.

8. נַסֵּה לְהָרִיחַ פֶּרַח.

9. מְצָא בַּכִּתָּה חֵפֶץ שֶׁאַתָּה אוֹהֵב.

10. מְצָא מִסְפָּר שֶׁקָּטָן מֵעֶשֶׂר וְגָדוֹל מֵחָמֵשׁ.

11. מְצָא בַּכִּתָּה חֵפֶץ שֶׁאֶפְשָׁר לִתְלוֹת עַל הַקִּיר.

12. שִׂים רֶגֶל יָמִין עַל הָרֹאשׁ.

13. סְפֹר מִמִּסְפָּר 1 וְעַד 20 בְּעִבְרִית.

14. מְצָא חֵפֶץ יָרֹק.

15. עֲנֵה: מִי הֲכִי גָּבוֹהַּ בַּכִּתָּה.

16. מְצָא שֵׁם שֶׁל סֵפֶר שֶׁמַּתְחִיל בָּאוֹת ה.

17. עֲנֵה מַהֵר: שֵׁם שֶׁל אֶרֶץ שֶׁמַּתְחִיל בָּאוֹת א.

18. מְצָא חֵפֶץ בַּכִּתָּה שֶׁמַּתְחִיל בָּאוֹת מ.

19. שֵׁב עַל הָרִצְפָּה.

20. שִׂים שְׁתֵּי יָדַיִם עַל הָרֹאשׁ וּקְפֹץ עֶשֶׂר פְּעָמִים.

* ההנחיות לעיל נזכרות בלשון זכר מטעמי נוחות בלבד.

Jerusalem has been called by many names. Here are some examples. Pick one and try to draw or write few words that describe the title you chose.

Covenant of God	בְּרִית-אֵל
The center of the world	מֶרְכַּז הָעוֹלָם
Zion fortress	מְצוּדַת צִיוֹן
Capital City	עִיר הַבִּירָה
Heroic City	עִיר הַגְּבוּרָה
City of God	עִיר הָאֱלֹקִים
City of Peace	עִיר הַשָּׁלוֹם
City of Strength	עִיר הָעֹז
City of Truth	עִיר הָאֱמֶת
The Wailing Wall	עִיר הַחוֹמָה - הַכֹּתֶל
City of Justice	עִיר הַצֶּדֶק
The Holy City	עִיר הַקֹּדֶשׁ

שִׂיחָה עִם אֱלֹקִים

If I could talk to God I would.....

מְסַפֵּר/ מְסַפֶּרֶת לוֹ שֶ...

_____

_____

_____

_____

_____

מְבַקֵּשׁ/ מְבַקֶּשֶׁת מִמֶּנּוּ שֶ...

_____

_____

_____

_____

_____

מַצִּיעַ/ מַצִּיעָה שֶ...

_____

_____

_____

_____

_____

לְבַסּוֹף, הָיִיתִי מוֹדֶה /מוֹדָה לוֹ עַל...

_____

_____

_____

_____

_____

אוֹצַר מִלִּים

Draw a small picture for each one of the following items:

מַתָּנָה	יְלָדִים	חֻלְצָה	חָבֵר
תַּפּוּחַ-אֲדָמָה	תִּירָס	שָׁטִיחַ	לַיְלָה
לֶחֶם	מִשְׁקָפַיִם	גֶּזֶר	סָלָט
אָזְנַיִם	מַחְשֵׁב	פֶּה	רֹאשׁ
מַגָּפַיִם	שָׁעוֹן	פְּרָחִים	עֵינַיִם

101 - Let's have fun

Roni Rosenthal-Gazit

LaVergne, TN USA
15 March 2010
176047LV00001B/2/P

9 780979 280016